Sources of Civilization in the West

Crane Brinton and Robert Lee Wolff,
General Editors

Sydney W. Jackman, the editor of this volume, **is** Associate Professor of History at the University of Victoria in British Columbia. He received his degrees from the University of Washington and Harvard University. A Fellow of the Royal Historical Society, he was a Rockefeller Fellow for research in the ideas of Lord Bolingbroke at Clare College, Cambridge, 1961-1962. Dr. Jackman is the author of *Galloping Head: The Life of Sir Francis Bond Head* and *With Burgoyne from Quebec*. He has edited Frederick Marryat's *A Diary in America* and has contributed numerous articles to historical journals.

ALREADY PUBLISHED

The Crisis of Church & State, 1050-1300, *by Brian Tierney (with selected documents)*, S-102

The English Reform Tradition, 1790-1910, *edited by Sydney W. Jackman*, S-120

The Enlightenment, *edited by Frank E. Manuel*, S-121

FORTHCOMING VOLUMES

The Ancient World, *edited by Zeph Stewart*

The Renaissance, *edited by Werner Gundersheimer*

The Protestant Reformation, *edited by Lewis Spitz*

The Catholic Reformation, *edited by Theodore K. Rabb*

The French Revolution, *edited by Philip Dawson*

Nineteenth-Century Intellectual History, *edited by Richard L. Schoenwald*

THE ENGLISH
REFORM TRADITION
1790-1910

Edited by

Sydney W. Jackman

Gather, O gather,
Foeman and Friend in love and peace!
Waves sleep together
When the blasts that called them to battle, cease.
For fangless Power, grown tame and mild
Is at play with Freedom's fearless child—
The dove and the serpent reconciled.

Percy Bysshe Shelley

PRENTICE-HALL, INC.

A SPECTRUM BOOK *Englewood Cliffs, New Jersey*

Current printing (last digit):

11 10 9 8 7 6 5 4 3

To
Lucretia P. Cameron-Head
of
Inverailort

Mountains divide us, and the waste of seas—
. . . but I in dreams behold the Hebrides.

FOREWORD

Between the late eighteenth and the late nineteenth centuries Great Britain achieved without major violence the kind of transition from government by a privileged few to government by something very close to universal suffrage that was achieved elsewhere in the Western world only by revolution. This process—sometimes called by historians of the thirteen colonies of British North America, which became by revolution the United States of America, a "progress from subject to citizen"—took place a century later in the mother country without revolution. It is true that the *form* of ceremonial monarchy was retained in Britain: indeed in the mid-twentieth century English, Scottish, and Welsh in the homeland are still "British subjects." But in all that counts beyond legal formalities they are in fact "British citizens."

Just as a case history, then, of the peaceful attainment of democracy, the development Professor Jackman spreads before the reader from contemporary documents in this book is of great importance to us today. For the whole world is now undergoing what is sometimes called "the revolution of rising expectations" or simply "modernization." This process of social change is bewilderingly complex. Whether or not it will end in the establishment of truly democratic societies all over the globe no sensible person would dare try to predict. The best we can do is to try to understand, partly with the help of the experience the study of history affords us, some of the conditions under which democracy has developed, and seems therefore not unlikely to develop in the future. For this purpose the documents Professor Jackman has here assembled, together with his own explanatory notes and introduction, should afford the reader a most useful exercise in training his mind, in forming him to use his judgment on these high and difficult matters of world politics. For the citizen, in contrast to the subject, is obliged to think and to judge for himself. If he does not do so, he is no more than a subject, perhaps, unfortunately, less.

Crane Brinton
Professor of History
Harvard University

CONTENTS

INTRODUCTION

> It was the best of times, it was the worst of times, it was the age of wisdom, it was the age of foolishness, it was the epoch of belief, it was the epoch of incredulity, it was the season of Light, it was the season of Darkness, it was the spring of hope, it was the winter of despair, we had everything before us, we had nothing before us, we were all going direct to heaven, we were all going direct the other way—in short, the period was so like the present period . . . it was clearer than crystal to the lords of the State preservers of loaves and fishes that things in general were settled forever.

> Charles Dickens, *A Tale of Two Cities*

The nineteenth century in England, like all ages, was an age of contradiction. The men and women of that century were like men and women who lived in the century before and in the century following. Their hopes, their despairs, their joys, their sadnesses were similar to those experienced by people everywhere. Nevertheless, it is possible to isolate some striking national characteristics that distinguish the Englishmen of the nineteenth century.

First, by the end of the eighteenth century the English had experienced an economic revolution which gave them very distinct advantages in the world of commerce and industry. It is true that other nations had or were having similar economic revolutions, but none was so complete nor of such magnitude as the English. Second, and definitely related to the economic revolution, an agricultural revolution had radically altered the structure of English rural society. Third, the English had basically settled their form of government; kings continued to reign but they ruled less; the sovereignty of Parliament was accepted and the government, although still in many ways the Crown's servant, was actually responsible to the national legislature. Fourth, there had been a revolution of spirit. This had manifested itself in two directions. There was the religious revivalism of Wesleyanism and Anglican evangelicalism which directed men not only to think of their own salvation but also to have a concern for man and his lot here on earth and to seek means of alleviating his distresses as much as possible. The other revolution of spirit, the Romantic movement, was also in its way religious but without a formal deity or theology. It was concerned with freeing man's spirit, providing him with a new way of looking at the world, and giving him newly formulated humanistic values. All of these revolutions profoundly affected English life in the nineteenth century and provided, in varying degrees, the sources of inspiration for the radical changes and reforms of that century.

To their enemies the English were "the nation of shopkeepers," for they prided themselves on their ledger-books, their banks, their credit, and their dividends. If Ebenezer Scrooge was to many a real villain for his treatment of his clerk Bob Cratchit, at the same time he embodied much that was accounted virtuous. Money and the possession of it were good; national prosperity was a grace bestowed on a kind of Calvinist elect. At the same time other, and seemingly contradictory, forces were also in evidence—these distinctly lessened the significance of the business ethic. Although money and commerce were in themselves good, status came not so much from the possession of capital as from the possession of land. Thus, the English were at the same time modern and feudal. Indeed, all the internal conflicts of England in the first half of the nineteenth century, and perhaps even later, constituted a kind of epic struggle between landlords and manufacturers, between the spirit of feudalism and that of commerce. The English were a practical people and an idealistic people, and their pragmatism frequently ran afoul of their idealism.

Not everyone agreed on the nature of the constitution and the role of government. A few pure Burkeans regarded the constitution and its operation as fixed and immutable. Others, and again these were a minority, thought the constitution should change and progress. The mass of society did not bother to philosophize on the nature of government but rather accepted it. Certain special aspects of the view of government, however, were common to holders of all these attitudes. Although outwardly English life was relatively free from *Jacqueries,* the mob periodically got out of control and started shouting for the traditional rights of Englishmen; for the Englishman then as now was passionately concerned with what he deemed to be his rights. If he did not have an intellectual grasp of them, he did know, apparently instinctively, what his rights were, and he was determined that no government should deprive him of them. Even so, no political faction was able to make full use of mob action, since at the same time revolutionary violence was somehow felt to limit traditional English rights.

The revolt of conscience had its direct influence. The Wesleyan or Methodist movement turned some of the national energy, particularly that of the lower classes, to religion when otherwise it might have sought outlet in political action. Elie Halevy, the great French historian and student of English history, very definitely credits this religious movement with having prevented the ideas of the French Revolution from taking hold in England. John Wesley was a Tory of Tories, and not a single sermon of the nearly fifty thousand that he delivered in his life expressed anything but loyalty to the monarchy and acceptance of the *status quo.* However, a spirit of charity was ever present in him and he advocated humanitarian ideals; these ideals were later to be translated from charitable actions into political reforms.

The Anglican Church, which was also a bulwark of Toryism, was awakening from its torpor, and some of its members showed an active social conscience. The most prominent among these Anglicans were those who associated with William Wilberforce, such as Zachary Macaulay and Granville Sharp—a group later known as "the Clapham Sect." So influential were they that they enlisted the support of the prime minister, William Pitt, in the greatest of their reforms, the abolition of the slave trade.

"The Clapham Sect" and the Wesleyan Methodists came from widely differing social strata, but they had many aims in common. Both were concerned for the poor, the homeless, and the neglected. Both undertook to improve society—not on the basis of eighteenth-century rationalism and human perfectibility but rather as Christian duty. Their descendants were to be the strongest supporters of Lord

Shaftesbury's attempts to alleviate the working conditions of women and children. They were indirectly the progenitors of Christian socialism* and settlement houses and temperance hotels. From their influence came the custom of family prayers and the gradual diminution of rustic vulgarity and cruelty.

Above all, the English had never acquired a nobility that became a closed circle as had nations on the Continent. Few members of the aristocracy could claim noble ancestry before the sixteenth century, and most were of much more recent vintage. It was possible for a prime minister to come from good mercantile stock and in due course become a peer. The new aristocracy quickly assumed the vices and the virtues of their fellow nobles and acquired the necessary status symbols and attitudes. The English upper classes had a long tradition of obligation toward the state and also toward the lower classes. Although the social standings of the upper and lower classes were widely separated, their interests were not unconnected. Nor was their association merely that of landlord and tenant; although the squire owned the land and the yeoman worked for him, they had many common bonds, some very strong. The squire—and this was a remnant of the feudal pattern of English life—was expected to look out for his men, be it in the hunting field or at the market. The English rural worker was not the European peasant. The new peers soon found that it was to their advantage to take on local coloration if only to be accepted socially, and what was perhaps initially self-interest became in time custom. In addition, Dr. Arnold's reforms in upper class education further enhanced this concept of obligation toward society.

To many the essential source of positive change, as in the past, was the government. The Constitutional Experiment of King George III really ended with Lord North's retirement and Dunning's resolution, "The power of the Crown is increasing, has increased, and ought to be diminished." The ministry, nominally still the royal servants, were actually servants of Parliament. In the

---

* Christian socialism, led by Charles Kingsley and Frederick Maurice, believed Christianity was a way of life and was concerned for the well-being of society. Slum clearance, education and sanitation were all taken up by the Christian Socialists. They based their actions on the teachings of the Christian religion and not purely on utilitarianism.

decade before the outbreak of the French Revolution Englishmen talked of parliamentary reform. Some, influenced by the American Revolution, felt that the colonists had been right in their refutation of the theory of "virtual representation"; others thought that Parliament had failed in its obligations to the country. These reformers were not wild radicals, but came from the gentry and upper middle classes. William Pitt himself advocated some kind of parliamentary reform and a wider degree of representation. However, the French Revolution, especially in its more radical aspects, ended these suggestions of reform. A few die-hards like Charles James Fox continued to support them, but Fox had few followers. The moderates were frightened into the camp of the reactionaries, and the whole country became increasingly conservative in spirit. Even the masses became politically apathetic or actually reactionary. Did not the mob, supported by the preachings of conservative clergy, sack the house of Joseph Priestley, the scientist, intellectual radical, and Unitarian in religion?

Although the writ of *habeas corpus* might be suspended and men could be transported for long periods of penal servitude for sedition, some reforms were still possible. In 1802 the elder Sir Robert Peel, a wealthy manufacturer and industrialist, had legislation passed under his sponsorship to protect apprentices and other young workers. This was the first real factory act. In addition, in 1807 the slave trade in the British Empire was formally abolished. These reforms may seem at first glance relatively insignificant, but it must be remembered that England at the time was involved in a twenty-year struggle with France. Moreover, these reforms, small in themselves, were like the first flowers in spring—a promise of what was to come when the climate moderated.

With the formal culmination of the war against France, when Europe was dominated by the spirit of the Holy Alliance, the English conservative was in no way a thorough-going reactionary. Of course the conservative feared the radical, and the establishment was able to absolve the authorities whose stupidity led to the Peterloo Massacre, and they approved of the notorious Six Acts limiting personal freedoms and the traditional rights of Englishmen. Even so, the press was not censored, criticism was permitted, and, although arrests were made, all the usual protection guaranteed by the law was still in effect; England never resorted to the repressive measures employed on the Continent.

Slowly the fears of the conservatives began to dissipate and the Tories, largely under the influence of the second Sir Robert Peel, George Canning, William Wilberforce, and William Huskisson, became more liberal. In the 1820s a whole spate of reforms was introduced, largely economic but also social, such as the final repeal of the Test and Corporation Acts. Upon the death of King George IV, with the accession of King William IV and the ensuing election, the old guard was swept from office, and after nearly half a century of opposition the Whigs under Lord Grey took office. The great ministry of Lord Grey and his successor Lord Melbourne probably made changes in English life more profound than those of any other two prime ministers previously or also perhaps subsequently.

With the passage of the Reform Bill of 1832, which extended the suffrage to the more affluent members of the middle class and changed the representation from many of the old rural boroughs to the industrial towns, the way was opened for many other reforms long overdue. The Whigs, many of whom had been nourished on the writings of Jeremy Bentham and the Utilitarian philosophy, concentrated their efforts in the social and legal spheres. The Whigs, although oligarchical and feudal in many ways, had come to be the spokesmen for and the protectors of the commercial interests; and this shift of political interest exemplified yet another aspect of the continuing struggle between the older rural, feudalistic society and the rising commercial class of the nineteenth century.

This struggle reached its climax when a Tory, Sir Robert Peel, (the younger) overthrew feudalism for conscience' sake, repealing those last remnants of protection, the Corn Laws, thereby reducing the cost of flour and bread. Naturally this pleased the employers, who could now pay lower wages, but their temporary gains were more than outweighed by the principle of government control which had now been established for good. Both Whigs and Tories had investigated conditions in mines and in industry; the poor climbing boys—so poignantly depicted by the poet Blake in his *The Little Black Boy*—the chimney sweeps' apprentices, had become objects of concern to the whole nation; the scandal of working conditions for women and pauper children had become the object of shame to the country. Cobden might assert that a nice warm factory was better than wet fields as a place to work but society, while perhaps agreeing with these sentiments, was determined that the employer should not have a totally free hand over his employees in either factory or field. The evangelical or Victorian conscience had come into full bloom.

Although the government was willing to extend its interest into the economic and social life of the country by making necessary reforms, it set itself firmly against further extensions of the national franchise. Lord John Russell, who had introduced the 1832 Reform Bill into the Commons, had acquired the sobriquet of "Finality Jack" because he declared that no further political reform was needed; however, his position was not accepted by much of the country and the late 1830s and early 1840s saw the rise of the Chartists. The aims of this group were relatively moderate and they sought only to bring more political democracy to England. The ruling classes, however, saw the Chartists as dangerous radicals and incipient revolutionaries, the upshot being that the Chartist movement, unlike its contemporary, the Anti-Corn Law League, was doomed to failure. Not until the next generation were any political reforms made.

If political reform was, for the moment at least, dead, social reform was not. The Victorians were nothing if not thorough; once they undertook a task they followed it through to what they deemed its logical conclusion. The Victorian Englishman, like Frederick in *The Pirates of Penzance,* was "a slave to duty." He was not above making a good profit, but he had his principles. Florence Nightingale's efforts to improve hospitals and public health generally were soon widely applauded. A concern for the poor became fashionable. Of course, public life did not immediately improve—slums there were a-plenty in the great industrial cities, hospitals continued to be unsanitary, and social welfare agencies were inadequate—but there was an ever-growing concern for human welfare. Literature and the press dealt more and more with the life and problems of ordinary people; the gulf between the social classes, while still vast, was decreasing little by little.

Following the death of Lord Palmerston in 1865, the old Whig

Party was transformed into the Liberal Party. William Ewart Gladstone, "the people's William," who became the new leader, symbolized the later Victorian reformer. Under his leadership legislation was passed improving public education, the civil service was based on competitive examination, the universities of Oxford and Cambridge were opened to men of all religious beliefs, the army was modernized and humanized, the secret ballot was introduced, the law courts were reformed, and the franchise was extended. The Liberals were not the only group concerned with reform. The Tories, or Conservatives as they called themselves, took up the reforming tradition as well. Under the inspired leadership of Benjamin Disraeli with his doctrine of "Tory Democracy," the party promoted legislation in public health, slum clearance, and similar areas of interest.

However, the Victorians were not able to overcome many of their inherent prejudices; they failed to see how all these reforms were leading to a completely secular society. Although the country had never been violently anti-Semitic, Jews were not given full political rights until 1858; more significant perhaps was the crisis caused by the election of Charles Bradlaugh to Parliament. England looked upon itself as tolerant of others but basically a Christian nation. Bradlaugh was an atheist, and Parliament refused to allow him to take his seat when he would not take the necessary oaths on a Bible. Only after much difficulty was he finally seated—some six years after his initial election. Accompanying this steadily increasing secularization were demands for the disestablishment of the Anglican Church; this was carried out in Ireland and proposed for Wales but not enacted; in England, despite much criticism, the Church managed to retain its position, for the country was not yet ready for such extreme measures.

Even the crown came in for some criticism. Queen Victoria's long period of mourning for Prince Albert, when she almost disappeared from public life, combined with the rather indiscreet way of life led by the Prince of Wales, made some ask if the day of monarchy were not perhaps over. The socialists were among the more ardent critics of the throne, and if their numbers were not large they were influential in intellectual circles. The late 1870s and early 1880s saw the rise of the Social Democratic Federation and the Fabian Society, which in their separate ways expressed some of the sentiments of the new age. People were less and less willing to have decisions made from above or reforms imposed. Both political parties attempted, with varying degrees of success, to undermine these numerically small but vocal critics.

The increase of popular education enabled the working classes to read and to learn more about government. They began to translate their demands into political action and hard-core socialism gained a number of recruits. The Independent Labour Party was created in 1893 and the Labour Representation Committee was formed seven years later. These new Socialist parties lacked the sentimentality of the earlier Christian Socialists, but many who had supported the earlier movement became active in the practical politics of the working classes. By the last decade of the century the "Victorian compromise" was at an end.

When the Liberal Party won the election of 1905 the nineteenth-century reform movement had reached its climax. The new ministry under the leadership of Sir Henry Campbell-Bannerman, while containing remnants of the older liberal tradition, also counted among its membership such men as John Morley, John Burns, the first artisan to achieve cabinet rank, and David Lloyd George, "the Welsh Wizard." Indeed, Lloyd George became the spokesman of the new age; the ordinary man, the common man in the street, had triumphed over Whig oligarchs, Tory aristocrats, county squires, and Anglican clerics.

The new view of society assumed not only popular democracy in terms of universal manhood suffrage but also other governmental obligations besides governing. The Liberal Party had promised larger benefits under workmen's compensation, an old age pension scheme, better educational facilities, public housing, and improved sanitation; all of these were expensive. Facing a large deficit, the government altered the tax structure so that the possessors rather than the producers of wealth would bear the heavier burden. In the form of income and inheritance taxes, assessments on unearned income and unearned increments of land, and heavy rates on monopolies, these new levies were the means devised by the government to pay for social reforms. The rich, who had generally, albeit often grudgingly, accepted earlier reforms, rebelled, and rejected the budget in the House of Lords.

The Liberal government reacted sharply; on December 2, 1909,

Herbert Asquith, the prime minister, moved and carried a resolution in the Commons: "That the action of the House of Lords
in refusing to pass into law the financial provisions made by this
House for the service of the year is a breach of the Constitution and
a usurpation of the rights of the Commons." It was now war to
the knife. The reactionaries and their supporters in the Lords had
failed to recollect the warning issued by Disraeli many years previously that the upper chamber with its permanent conservative
majority should never allow itself to reject totally measures that
had the overwhelming approval of the Commons. Asquith and his
colleagues, following two general elections, managed to get the
Parliament Act passed by the summer of 1911. With the acceptance
of this great piece of legislation it might well be said that the age
of reform was over. From then on the people could ensure through
their representatives that the conservative forces could never permanently halt reforms demanded by the spirit of the time.

All of this had come about without real revolutionary violence.
A number of explanations, taken together, help indicate why this
was so. At the beginning of the nineteenth century the work of
John Wesley probably deflected some energy away from political
agitation and into religious enthusiasm. The long war against
Napoleon also prevented political agitation by directing national
energy to the prosecution of the war and by glorifying patriotism. In
the years immediately following Napoleon's downfall the government may have been harsh but it was never tyrannical and social
conditions were never unbearable. When the fears of the establishment were diminished its members themselves became reformers;
indeed the activities of Peel and Huskisson followed by those of
Grey and his colleagues demonstrate the aristocracy's sensible conviction that it is better to reform from above than to be reformed
from below. The ruling classes, to paraphrase Disraeli, "caught the
revolutionaries bathing and ran off with their clothes." At no time
did the government fail to give in to national desires for reform;
it sometimes resisted purely class desires, but not national aspi-
rations reflecting the wishes of the majority. Another reason for the
lack of violence might well be the great dearth of charismatic revolutionary leaders. Most of the leaders of the period were respectable
figures committed to traditional patterns of reform; the few that

belonged to the lunatic fringe were dismissed by the British public. Moreover, if one simply could not bear conditions at home, one could always emigrate, and many of those who might have played major roles in revolutionary activity went to Canada, or Australia, or New Zealand; in the colonies there was more democracy, if not politically at least socially. National prosperity also undoubtedly helped prevent forcible revolution. At no time did acute economic need drive society to take over the means of production and the government of the state. At the end of the century the trade unions, the socialist movements, and the Fabian Society emphasized evolution rather than revolution, playing a role similar to that of the Wesleyan movement in deflecting violence. Finally—and this is perhaps part of the British character—violent revolution was generally considered something continental and "foreign." Foreign ideas and customs were inferior to good British traditions, and the English felt no need to copy their neighbors.

If the conflict in the early nineteenth century was between the forces of feudalism and the forces of commercialism, then at the end of the era—including the reign of King Edward VII—the conflict was between the forces of privilege and wealth and the forces of democracy. It is evident that the second grew out of the first; the later struggle was inevitable from the moment in 1832 when the Reform Bill became law, and perhaps even earlier, when the government assumed jurisdiction over private property such as slaves or over such aspects of public welfare as poverty and conditions of employment. Society was to be concerned for all men, not just for the privileged few. In an odd way, and not quite in the same context but expressing the correct sentiments, one of the Social Darwinists summed up the situation very neatly: "The path of progress is strewn with the wrecks of nations; traces are everywhere to be seen of the hecatombs of inferior races, and of victims who found not the narrow way to the greater perfection. Yet, these dead peoples are, in very truth, the stepping stones on which mankind has arisen to the higher intellectual and deeper emotional life of to-day."

One

THE INIQUITY
OF SLAVERY

William Pitt

William Pitt (1759-1806), statesman, was at twenty-five the youngest man ever to become prime minister of England. He always felt himself a disciple of his father William Pitt, Earl of Chatham, and thought he was in the great Whig tradition. However, others generally thought him a Tory, and he is so considered by the modern Conservative Party. Pitt was vitally interested in reform at the outset of his career and at one time advocated some degree of parliamentary reform. He was associated with many improvements in the financial administration of the country—for example, he created the "sinking fund" to help pay off the national debt. Pitt's circle included many who were also interested in humanitarianism; he was a great friend of William Wilberforce, Granville Sharp, and Thomas Clarkson. It was his intimacy with these men that led him to support their anti-slavery program. The first step was the abolition of the slave trade and it was on this issue that Pitt spoke on April 2, 1792, addressing the House of Commons in support of a motion introduced by Wilberforce. The prime minister's prestige did much to help the passage of the bill ending the slave trade; unfortunately legal and constitutional complications kept the bill from coming into full force until 1807. This speech by Pitt is one of his greatest; it demonstrates not only his personal sentiments on the question of Negro slavery, but also the power that he had as a speaker and leader of his party. *The Speech of the Right Hon. William Pitt on a Motion for the Abolition of the Slave Trade in the House of Commons on Monday the Second of April, 1792* (London, Phillips, 1792).

At this hour of the morning I am afraid, Sir, I am too much exhausted to enter so fully into the subject before the committee as I could wish; but if my bodily strength is in any degree equal to the task, I feel so strongly the magnitude of this question that I am extremely earnest to deliver my sentiments, which I rise to do with the more satisfaction, because I now look forward to the issue of this business with considerable hopes of success. The debate has this day taken a turn which, though it has produced a variety of new suggestions, has, upon the whole, reduced this question to a much narrower point than it was ever brought into before. I cannot say that I quite agree with the right hon. gentleman over the way [Mr. Fox]; I am far from deploring all that has been said by my two hon. friends [Mr. Dundas and the Speaker]; I rather rejoice that they have now brought this subject to a fair issue—that something, at least, is already gained, and that the argument has taken altogether a new course this night. It is true, a difference of opinion has been stated, and has been urged with all the force of argument that could be given to it. But give me leave to say, that this difference has been urged upon principles very far removed from those which were maintained by the opponents of my hon. friend when he first brought forward his motion. There are very few of those who have spoken this night who have not declared the abolition of the slave trade to be their ultimate object. The point now in dispute between us is a difference merely as to the time at which the abolition ought to take place. I therefore congratulate this House, the country, and the world, that this great point has been gained; that we may now consider this trade as having received its condemnation; that this curse of mankind is seen by the House in its true light; that this stigma on our national character is about to be removed; and that mankind are likely to be delivered from the greatest practical evil that ever afflicted the human race—from the severest and most extensive calamity recorded in the history of the world.

In proceeding to give my reasons for concurring with my hon. friend in his motion, I shall necessarily advert to those topics which my right hon. friends near me have touched upon, and which they stated to be their motives for preferring a gradual abolition to the more immediate and direct measure now proposed. Beginning as

I do, with declaring that in this respect I differ completely from my right hon. friends near me, I do not, however, mean to say that I differ as to one observation which has been pressed rather strongly by them. If they can show that by proceeding gradually we shall arrive more speedily at our end than by a direct vote immediately to abolish; if they can show that our proposition has more the appearance of a speedy abolition than the reality; undoubtedly they will in this case make a convert of every man among us who looks to this as a question not to be determined by theoretical principles or enthusiastic feelings, but considers the practicability of the measure—aiming simply to effect his object in the shortest time, and in the surest possible manner. If, however, I shall be able to show that the slave trade will on our plan be abolished sooner than on theirs, may I not then hope that my right hon. friends will be as ready to adopt our proposition as we should in the other case be willing to accede to theirs? One of my right hon. friends has stated that an Act passed here for the abolition of the slave trade would not secure its abolition. Now, Sir, I should be glad to know why an act of the British legislature, enforced by all those sanctions which we have undoubtedly the power and the right to apply, is not to be effectual, at least as to every material purpose. Will not the executive power have the same appointment of the officers and the courts of judicature, by which all the causes relating to this subject must be tried, that it has in other cases? Will there not be the same system of law by which we now maintain a monopoly of commerce? If the same law, Sir, be applied to the prohibition of the slave trade which is applied in the case of other contraband commerce, with all the same means of the country to back it, I am at a loss to know why the total abolition is not as likely to be effected in this way, as by any project of my right hon. friends for bringing about a gradual termination of it. But my observation is strongly fortified by what fell from my hon. friend who spoke last. He has told you, Sir, that if you will have patience with it for a few years, the slave trade must drop of itself, from the increasing dearness of the commodity imported, and the increasing progress, on the other hand, of internal population. Is it true, then, that the importations are so expensive and disadvantageous already that the internal population is even now becoming a cheaper resource? I ask, then, if you leave to the importer no means of importation but by smuggling, and if, besides all the present disadvantages, you load him with all the charges and hazards of the smuggler, by taking care that the laws against smuggling are in this case rigorously enforced, is there any danger of any considerable supply of fresh slaves being poured into the islands through this channel? And is there any real ground of fear, because a few slaves may have been smuggled in or out of the islands, that a bill will be ineffectual on any such ground? The question under these circumstances will not bear a dispute.

Perhaps, however, my hon. friends may take up another ground and say, "It is true your measure would shut out further importations more immediately; but we think it right, on grounds of general expediency, that they should not be immediately shut out." Let us come then to this question of the expediency of making the abolition distant and gradual rather than immediate. The argument of expediency, in my opinion, will not justify the continuance of the slave trade for one unnecessary hour. Supposing it to be in our power (which I have shown it is) to enforce the prohibition from this present time, the expediency of doing it is to me so clear that, if I went on this principle alone, I should not feel a moment's hesitation. What is the argument of expediency stated on the other side? It is doubted whether the deaths and births in the islands are as yet so nearly equal as to ensure the keeping up of a sufficient stock of labourers. In answer to this, I took the liberty of mentioning, in a former year, what appeared to me to be the state of population at that time. My observations were taken from documents which we have reason to judge authentic, and which carried on the face of them the conclusions I then stated: they were the clear, simple, and obvious result of a careful examination which I made into this subject, and any gentleman who will take the same pains may arrive at the same degree of satisfaction. These calculations, however, applied to a period of time that is now four or five years past. The births were then, in the general view of them, nearly equal to the deaths; and, as the state of population was shown by a considerable retrospect to be regularly increasing, an excess of births must before this time have taken place. Another observation has been made as to the disproportion of the sexes. This, however, is a disparity which will gradually diminish as the slave-trade diminishes, and must entirely cease when the trade shall be abolished. I believe this disproportion of the sexes is not now by any means considerable. But, Sir, I also showed that the great mortality which turned the balance so as to make the deaths appear more numerous than the births, arose too from the imported Africans, who die in extraordinary numbers in the seasoning. If, therefore, the importation of negroes should cease, every one of the causes of mortality which I have now stated would cease also. Nor can I conceive any reason why the present number of labourers should not maintain itself in the West Indies, except it be from some artificial cause, some fault in the islands; such as the impolicy of their governors, or the cruelty of the managers and officers whom they employ. I will not repeat all that I said at that time, or go through island by island. It is true, there is a difference in the ceded islands; and I state them possibly to be, in some respects, an excepted case. But, if we are to enter into the subject of the mortality in clearing new lands, this, Sir, is undoubtedly another question; the mortality here is tenfold: and this is to be considered, not as the carrying on of a trade, but as the setting on foot of a slave trade for the purpose of peopling the colony; a measure which I think will not now be maintained. I therefore desire gentlemen to tell me fairly, whether the period they look to is not now arrived? Whether, at this hour, the West Indies may not be declared to have actually attained a state in which they can maintain their population? And upon the answer I must necessarily receive, I think I could safely rest the whole of the question.

One hon. gentleman has rather ingeniously observed that one or other of these two assertions of ours must necessarily be false: that either the population must be decreasing, which we deny; or if the population is increasing, that the slaves must be perfectly well treated (this being the cause of such population), which we deny also. That the population is rather increasing than otherwise, and also that the general treatment is by no means so good as it ought to be, are both points which have been separately proved by different evidences; nor are these two points so entirely incompatible. The ill-treatment must be very great indeed in order to diminish materially the population of any race of people. That it is not so extremely great as to do this, I will admit. I will even admit that this charge may possibly have been sometimes exaggerated; and I certainly think that it applies less and less as we come nearer to the present times. But let us see how this contradiction of ours, as it is thought, really stands, and how the explanation of it will completely settle our minds on the point in question. Do the slaves diminish in numbers? It can be nothing but ill-treatment that causes the diminution. This ill-treatment the abolition must and will restrain. In this case, therefore, we ought to vote for the abolition. On the other hand, do you choose to say that the slaves clearly increase in numbers? Then you want no importations, and, in this case also, you may safely vote for the abolition. Or, if you choose to say, as the third and only other case which can be put, and which perhaps is the nearest to the truth, that the population is nearly stationary and the treatment neither so bad nor so good as it might be; then surely, Sir, it will not be denied that this of all others is, on each of the two grounds, the proper period for stopping further supplies; for your population, which you own is already stationary, will thus be made undoubtedly to increase from the births; and the good treatment of your present slaves, which I am now supposing is but very moderate, will be necessarily improved also by the same measure of abolition. I say, therefore, that these propositions, contradictory as they may be represented, are in truth not at all inconsistent, but even come in aid of each other, and lead to a conclusion that is decisive. And let it be always remembered, that in this branch of my argument I have only in view the well-being of the West Indies, and do not now ground anything on the African part of the question.

But, Sir, I may carry these observations respecting the islands much further. It is within the power of the colonists (and is it not then their indispensable duty?) to apply themselves to the correction of those various abuses by which population is restrained. The most important consequences may be expected to attend colonial regulations for this purpose. With the improvement of internal population, the condition of every negro will improve also; his liberty will advance, or at least he will be approaching to a state of liberty. Nor can you increase the happiness, or extend the freedom of the negro, without adding in an equal degree to the safety of the islands, and of all their inhabitants. Thus, Sir, in the place of slaves, who naturally have an interest directly opposite to that of their masters, and are therefore viewed by them with an eye of constant suspicion, you will create a body of valuable citizens and subjects, forming a part of the same community, having a common interest with their superiors, in the security and prosperity of the whole. And here let me add, that in proportion as you increase the happiness of these unfortunate beings, you will undoubtedly increase in effect the quantity of their labour also. Gentlemen talk of the diminution of the labour of the islands. I will venture to assert that, even if in consequence of the abolition there were to be some decrease in the number of hands, the quantity of work done, supposing the condition of the slaves to improve, would by no means diminish in the same proportion: perhaps would be far from diminishing at all. For if you restore to this degraded race the true feelings of men, if you take them out among the order of brutes, and place them on a level with the rest of the human species, they will then work with that energy which is natural to men, and their labour will be productive, in a thousand ways, above what it has yet been; as the labour of a man is always more productive than that of a mere brute.

It generally happens that in every bad cause some information arises out of the evidence of its defenders themselves, which serves to expose in one part or other the weakness of their defence. It is the characteristic of such a cause that if it be at all gone into, even by its own supporters, it is liable to be ruined by the contradictions in which those who maintain it are for ever involved. The committee of the privy council of Great Britain sent over certain queries to the West India islands, with a view of elucidating the present subject; and they particularly inquired, whether the negroes had any days or hours allotted to them in which they might work for themselves. The assemblies in their answers, with an air of great satisfaction, state the labour of the slaves to be moderate, and the West India system to be well calculated to promote the domestic happiness of the slaves: they add, "that proprietors are not compelled by law to allow their slaves any part of the six working days of the week for themselves, but that it is the general practice to allow them one afternoon in every week out of crop time, which, with such hours as they choose to work on Sundays, is time amply sufficient for their own purposes." Now, therefore, will the negroes, or I may rather say, do the negroes work for their own emolument? I beg the committee's attention to this point. The assembly of Grenada proceeds to state—I have their own words for it—"That though the negroes are allowed the afternoons of only one day in every week, they will do as much work in that afternoon, when employed for their own benefit, as in the whole day when employed in their master's service." Now, Sir, I will desire you to burn all my calculations; to disbelieve, if you please, every word I have said on the present state of population; nay, I will admit, for the sake of argument, that the numbers are decreasing, and the productive labour is at present insufficient for the cultivation of those countries: and I will then ask, whether the increase in the quantity of labour which is reasonably to be expected from the improved condition of the slaves is not, by the admission of the islands themselves, far more than sufficient to counter-balance any decrease which can be rationally apprehended from a defective state of their population? Why, Sir, a negro, if he works for himself, and not for a master, will do double work! This is their own account. If you will believe the planters, if you will believe the legislature of the islands, the productive labour of the colonies would, in case the negroes worked as free labourers instead of slaves, be literally doubled. Half the present labourers, on this supposition, would suffice for the whole cultivation of our islands on the present scale. I therefore confidently ask the House whether, in considering the whole of this question, we may not fairly look forward to an improvement in the condition of these unhappy and degraded beings, not only as an event desirable on the ground of humanity and political prudence, but also as a means of increasing very considerably indeed (even without any increasing population) the productive industry of the islands? When gentlemen are so nicely balancing the past and future means of cultivating the plantations, let me request them to put this argument into the scale; and the more they consider it, the more will they be satisfied that both the solidity of the principle which I have stated, and the fact which I have just quoted in the very words of the colonial legislature, will bear me out in every inference I have drawn. I think they will perceive also, that it is the undeniable duty of this House, on the grounds of true policy, immediately to sanction and carry into effect that system which ensures these important advantages, in addition to all those other inestimable blessings which follow in their train.

If, therefore, the argument of expediency, as applying to the West India islands, is the test by which this question is to be tried, I trust I have now established this proposition, namely, that whatever tends most speedily and effectually to meliorate the condition of the slaves is undoubtedly, on the ground of expediency, leaving justice out of the question, the main object to be pursued. That the immediate abolition of the slave trade will most eminently have this effect, and that it is the only measure from which this effect can in any considerable degree be expected, are points to which I shall presently come; but before I enter upon them, let me notice one or two further circumstances. We are told (and by respectable and well-informed persons) that the purchase of new negroes has been injurious instead of profitable to the planters themselves; so large a proportion of these unhappy wretches being found to perish in the seasoning. Writers well versed in this subject have even advised that, in order to remove the temptation which the slave trade offers to expend large sums in this injudicious way, the door of importation should be shut. This very plan which we now propose, the mischief of which is represented to be so great as to outweigh so many other momentous considerations, has actually been recommended by some of the best authorities, as a plan highly requisite to be adopted, on the very principle of advantage to the island; nay, not merely on that principle of general and political advantage on which I have already touched, but for the advantage of the very individuals who would otherwise be most forward in purchasing slaves. On the part of the West Indians it is urged, "The planters are in debt: they are already distressed; if you stop the slave trade, they will be ruined." Mr. Long, the celebrated historian of Jamaica, recommends the stopping of importations as a receipt for enabling the plantations which are embarrassed to get out of debt. Speaking of the usurious terms on which money is often borrowed for the purchase of fresh slaves, he advises "the laying of a duty equal to a prohibition on all negroes imported for the space of four or five years, except for re-exportation. Such a law," he proceeds to say, "would be attended with the following good consequences. It would put an immediate stop to these extortions; it would enable the planter to retrieve his affairs by preventing him from running in debt, either by renting or purchasing negroes; it would render such recruits less necessary, by the redoubled care he would be obliged to take of his present stock, the preservation of their lives and health; and lastly, it would raise the value of negroes in the island. A North American province, by this prohibition alone for a few years, from being deeply plunged in debt, has become independent, rich, and flourishing." On this authority of Mr. Long I rest the question whether the prohibition of further importations is that rash, impolitic, and completely ruinous measure which it is so confidently declared to be with respect to our West Indian plantations. I do not, however, mean, in thus treating this branch of the subject, absolutely to exclude the question of indemnification, on the supposition of possible disadvantages affecting the West Indies through the abolition of the slave trade. But when gentlemen set up a claim of compensation merely on those general allegations, which are all that I have yet heard from them, I can only answer, let them produce their case in a distinct and specific form; and if upon any practicable or reasonable grounds it shall claim consideration, it will then be time enough for Parliament to decide upon it.

I now come to another circumstance of great weight, connected with this part of the question—I mean the danger to which the islands are exposed from those negroes who are newly imported. This, Sir, is no more speculation of ours: for here again I refer you to Mr. Long. He treats particularly of the dangers to be dreaded from the introduction of Coromantine negroes—an appellation under which are comprised several descriptions of negroes obtained on the Gold Coast, whose native country is not exactly known, and who are purchased in a variety of markets, having been brought from some distance inland. With a view of preventing insurrections, he advises that "by laying a duty equal to a prohibition, no more of these Coromantines should be bought"; and after noticing one insurrection which happened through their means, he tells you of another in the following year, in which thirty-three Coromantines, "most of whom had been newly imported, suddenly rose, and in the space of an hour murdered and wounded no less than nineteen white persons." To the authority of Mr. Long I may add the recorded opinion of the committee of the house of assembly of Jamaica itself, who, in consequence of a rebellion among the slaves, were appointed to inquire into the best means of preventing future insurrections. The committee reported, "That the rebellion had originated (like most or all others) with the Coromantines; and they proposed that a bill should be brought in for laying a higher duty on the importation of these particular negroes," which was intended to operate as a prohibition. But the danger is not confined to the importation of Coromantines. Mr. Long, carefully investigating as he does the causes of such frequent insurrections, particularly at Jamaica, accounts for them from the greatness of its general importations. "In two years and a half," says he, "27,000 negroes have been imported. No wonder we have rebellions! 27,000 in two years and a half!" Why, Sir, I believe that in some late years there have been as many imported into the same island within the same period. Surely, when gentlemen talk so vehemently of the safety of the islands, and charge us with being so indifferent to it; when they speak of the calamities of St. Domingo, and of similar dangers impending over their own heads at the present hour, it ill becomes them to be the persons who are crying out for further importations. It ill becomes them to charge upon us the crime of stirring up insurrections—upon us who are only adopting the very principles which Mr. Long, which in part even the legislature of Jamaica itself, laid down in the time of danger, with an avowed view to the prevention of any such calamity.

It is no small satisfaction to me, Sir, that among the many arguments for prohibiting the slave trade which crowd upon my mind, the security of our West India possessions against internal commotions, as well as foreign enemies, is among the most prominent; and here let me apply to my two right hon. friends, and ask them whether in this part of the argument they did not see reason for immediate abolition? Why should you any longer import into those countries that which is the very seed of insurrection and rebellion? Why should you persist in introducing those latent principles of conflagration which, if they should once burst forth, may annihilate

in a single day the industry of a hundred years? Why will you subject yourselves, with open eyes, to the imminent risk of a calamity
which may throw you back a whole century in your profits, in your
cultivation, in your progress to the emancipation of your slaves?
and, disappointing at once every one of those golden expectations,
may retard not only the accomplishment of that happy system
which I have attempted to describe, but may cut off even your
opportunity of taking any one introductory step? Let us begin from
this time. Let us not commit these important interests to any
further hazard. Let us prosecute this great object from this very
hour. Let us vote that the abolition of the slave trade shall be immediate, and not left to I know not what future time or contin-
gency. Will my right hon. friends answer for the safety of the
islands during any imaginable intervening period? Or do they
think that any little advantages of the kind which they state can
have any weight in that scale of expediency in which this great
question ought undoubtedly to be tried? Thus stated, and thus
alone, Sir, can it be truly stated, to what does the whole of my right
hon. friend's arguments, on the head of expediency, amount? It
amounts but to this:—the colonies on the one hand would have to
struggle with some few difficulties and disadvantages at the first,
for the sake of obtaining on the other hand immediate security to
their leading interests; of ensuring, Sir, even their own political
existence; and for the sake also of immediately commencing that
system of progressive improvement in the condition of the slaves
which is necessary to raise them from the state of brutes to that of
rational beings, but which never can begin until the introduction
of these new disaffected and dangerous Africans into the same gangs
shall have been stopped.—If any argument can in the slightest
degree justify the severity that is now so generally practised in the
treatment of the slaves, it must be the introduction of these Africans. It is the introduction of these Africans that renders all idea of
emancipation for the present so chimerical, and the very mention
of it so dreadful. It is the introduction of these Africans that keeps
down the condition of all plantation negroes. Whatever system of
treatment is deemed necessary by the planters to be adopted towards
these new Africans, extends itself to the other slaves also. Instead,
therefore, of deferring the hour when you will finally put an end

to importations, vainly purposing that the condition of your present slaves should previously be mended, you must, in the very first instance, stop your importations, if you hope to introduce any rational or practicable plan either of gradual emancipation or present general improvement.

Having now done with this question of expediency as affecting the islands, I come next to a proposition advanced by my right hon. friend [Mr. Dundas], which appeared to intimate that on account of some patrimonial rights of the West Indians, the prohibition of the slave trade might be considered as an invasion on their legal inheritance. Now, in answer to this proposition, I must make two or three remarks, which I think my right hon. friend will find some considerable difficulty in answering.—First, I observe that his argument, if it be worth anything, applies just as much to gradual as immediate abolition. I have no doubt that at whatever period he should be disposed to say the abolition should actually take place, this defence will equally be set up; for it certainly is just as good an argument against an abolition seven, or seventy years hence, as against an abolition at this moment. It supposes we have no right whatever to stop the importations, and even though the disadvantage to our plantations, which some gentlemen suppose to attend the measure of immediate abolition, should be admitted gradually to lessen by the lapse of a few years, yet in point of principle the absence of all right of interference would remain the same. My right hon. friend, therefore, I am sure will not press an argument not less hostile to his proposition than to ours. But let us investigate the foundation of this objection, and I will commence what I have to say by putting a question to my right hon. friend. It is chiefly on the presumed ground of our being bound by a parliamentary sanction heretofore given to the African slave trade that this argument against the abolition is rested. Does, then, my right hon. friend think that the slave trade has received any such parliamentary sanction as must place it more out of the jurisdiction of the legislature for ever after, than the other branches of our national commerce? I ask, is there any one regulation of any part of our commerce which, if this argument be valid, may not equally be objected to, on the ground of its affecting some man's patrimony, some man's property, or some man's expectations? Let it never be forgotten that the argument I am canvassing would be just as strong if the possession affected were small, and the possessors humble; for on every principle of justice the property of any single individual, or small number of individuals, is as sacred as that of the great body of West Indians. Justice ought to extend her protection with rigid impartiality to the rich and to the poor, to the powerful and to the humble. If this be the case, in what a situation does my right hon. friend's argument place the legislature of Great Britain? What room is left for their interference in the regulation of any part of our commerce? It is scarcely possible to lay a duty on any one article which may not, when first opposed, be said in some way to affect the property of individuals, and even of some entire classes of the community. If the laws respecting the slave trade imply a contract for its perpetual continuance, I will venture to say there does not pass a year without some act, equally pledging the faith of parliament to the perpetuating of some other branch of commerce. In short, I repeat my observation, that no new tax can be imposed, much less can any prohibitory duty be ever laid on any branch of trade, that has before been regulated by parliament, if this principle be once admitted.

Before I refer to the acts of parliament by which the public faith is said to be pledged, let me remark also that a contract for the continuance of the slave trade must, on the principles which I shall presently insist on, have been void, even from the beginning; for if this trade is an outrage upon justice, and only another name for fraud, robbery, and murder, will any man urge that the legislature could possibly by any pledge whatever incur the obligation of being an accessory, or I may even say a principal, in the commission of such enormities, by sanctioning their countenance? As well might an individual think himself bound by a promise to commit an assassination. I am confident gentlemen must see that our proceedings on such grounds would infringe all the principles of law, and subvert the very foundation of morality.—Let us now see how far the acts themselves show that there is this sort of parliamentary pledge to continue the African slave trade. The act of 23d Geo. II., c. 31, is that by which we are supposed to be bound up by contract to sanction all those horrors now so incontrovertibly proved. How surprised then, Sir, must the House be to find that, by the clause of that very act, some of these outrages are expressly forbidden! It says, "No commander or master of a ship, trading to Africa, shall by fraud, force or violence, or by any indirect practice whatsoever, take on board or carry away from the coast of Africa any negro, or native of the said country, or commit any violence on the natives, to the prejudice of the said trade, and that every person so offending shall for every such offence forfeit"—When it comes to penalty, sorry am I to say that we see too close a resemblance to the West India law, which inflicts the payment of £30 as the punishment for murdering a negro. The price of blood in Africa is £100; but even this penalty is enough to prove that the act at least does not sanction, much less does it engage to perpetuate enormities.—But, Sir, let us see what was the motive for carrying on the trade at all. The preamble of the act states it, "Whereas the trade to and from Africa is very advantageous to Great Britain, and necessary for the supplying the plantations and colonies thereunto belonging with a sufficient number of negroes at reasonable rates, and for that purpose the said trade should be carried on," etc. Here, then, we see what the parliament had in view when it passed this act; and I have clearly shown that not one of the occasions on which it grounded its proceedings now exists. I may then plead, I think, the very act itself as an argument for the abolition. If it is shown that, instead of being "very advantageous" to Great Britain, this trade is the most destructive that can well be imagined to her interests; that it is the ruin of our seamen; that it stops the extension of our manufactures: if it is proved, in the second place, that it is not now necessary for the "supplying our plantations with negroes"; if it is further established that this traffic was from the very beginning contrary to the first principles of justice, and consequently that a pledge for its continuance, had one been attempted to have been given, must have been completely and absolutely void;—where then in this act of parliament is the contract to be found by which Britain is bound, as she is said to be, never to listen to her own true interests, and to the cries of the natives of Africa? Is it not clear that all argument, founded on the supposed pledged faith of parliament, makes against those who employ it? I refer you to the principles which obtain in other cases. Every trade act shows undoubtedly that the legislature is used to pay a tender regard to all classes of the community. But if, for the sake of moral duty, of national honour, or even of great political advantage, it is thought right . . . to alter any . . . system. . . . The legislature will . . . be careful to subject individuals to as little inconvenience as possible; and if any peculiar hardship should arise, that can be distinctly stated and fairly pleaded, there will ever, I am sure, be a liberal feeling towards them in the legislature of this country, which is the guardian of all who live under its protection. On the present occasion, the most powerful considerations call upon us to abolish the slave trade; and if we refuse to attend to them on the alleged ground of pledged faith and contract, we shall depart as widely from the practice of parliament as from the path of moral duty. If, indeed, there is any case of hardship, which comes within the proper cognisance of parliament, and calls for the exercise of its liberality,—well! But such a case must be reserved for calm consideration, as a matter distinct from the present question.

The result of all I have said is, that there exists no impediment, on the ground of pledged faith, or even on that of national expediency, to the abolition of this trade. On the contrary, all the arguments drawn from those sources plead for it, and they plead much more loudly, and much more strongly in every part of the question, for an immediate, than for a gradual abolition. But now, Sir, I come to Africa. That is the ground on which I rest, and here it is that I say my right hon. friends do not carry their principles to their full extent. Why ought the slave trade to be abolished? Because it is incurable injustice. How much stronger, then, is the argument for immediate, than gradual abolition! By allowing it to continue even for one hour, do not my right hon. friends weaken their own argument of its injustice? If on the ground of injustice it ought to be abolished at last, why ought it not now? Why is injustice to be suffered to remain for a single hour? From what I hear without doors, it is evident that there is a general conviction entertained of its being far from just; and from that very conviction of its injustice, some men have been led, I fear, to the supposition that the slave trade never could have been permitted to begin, but from some strong and irresistible necessity: a necessity, however, which if it was fancied to exist at first, I have shown cannot be thought by any man whatever to exist now. This plea of necessity has caused a sort of acquiescence in the continuance of this evil. Men have been led to place it among the rank of those necessary evils which are supposed to be the lot of human creatures, and to be permitted to fall upon some countries or individuals, rather than upon others, by that Being whose ways are inscrutable to us, and whose dispensations, it is conceived, we ought not to look into. The origin of evil is indeed a subject beyond the reach of human understandings: and the permission of it by the Supreme Being is a subject into which it belongs not to us to inquire. But where the evil in question is a moral evil which a man can scrutinise, and where the moral evil has its origin with ourselves, let us not imagine that we can clear our consciences by this general, not to say irreligious and impious, way of laying aside the question. If we reflect at all on this subject, we must see that every necessary evil supposes that some other and greater evil would be incurred were it removed. I therefore desire to ask, what can be that greater evil which can be stated to overbalance the one in question? I know of no evil that ever has existed, nor can imagine any evil to exist, worse than the tearing of seventy or eighty thousand persons annually from their native land, by a combination of the most civilised nations inhabiting the most enlightened part of the globe, but more especially under the sanction of the laws of that nation which calls herself the most free and the most happy of them all. Even if these miserable beings were proved guilty of every crime before you take them off, ought we to take upon ourselves the office of executioners? And even if we condescend so far, still can we be justified in taking them, unless we have clear proof that they are criminals?—But, if we go much further,—if we ourselves tempt them to sell their fellow-creatures to us,—we may rest assured that they will take care to provide by every possible method a supply of victims increasing in proportion to our demand. Can we, then, hesitate in deciding whether the wars in Africa are their wars or ours? It was our arms in the river Cameroon, put into the hands of the trader, that furnished him with the means of pushing his trade; and I have no more doubt that they are British arms, put into the hands of Africans, which promote universal war and desolation, than I can doubt their having done so in that individual instance.

I have shown how great is the enormity of this evil, even on the supposition that we take only convicts and prisoners of war. But take the subject in the other way, and how does it stand? Think of 80,000 persons carried out of their native country by we know not what means! for crimes imputed! for light or inconsiderable faults! for debt perhaps! for the crime of witchcraft! or a thousand other weak and scandalous pretexts! Reflect on these 80,000 persons thus annually taken off! There is something in the horror of it that surpasses all the bounds of imagination. Admitting that there exists in Africa something like to courts of justice; yet what an office of humiliation and meanness is it in us, to take upon ourselves to carry into execution the iniquitous sentences of such courts, as if we also were strangers to all religion, and to the first principles of justice! But that country, it is said, has been in some degree civilised, and civilised by us. It is said they have gained some knowledge of the principles of justice. Yes, we give them enough of our intercourse to convey to them the means, and to initiate them in the study of mutual destruction. We give them just enough of the forms of justice to enable them to add the pretext of legal trials to their other modes of perpetrating the most atrocious iniquity. We give them just enough of European improvements to enable them the more effectually to turn Africa into a ravaged wilderness. Some evidences say that the Africans are addicted to the practice of gambling; that they even sell their wives and children, and ultimately themselves. Are these, then, the legitimate sources of slavery? Shall we pretend that we can thus acquire an honest right to exact the labour of these people? Can we pretend that we have a right to carry away to distant regions men of whom we know nothing by authentic inquiry, and of whom there is every reasonable presumption to think that those who sell them to us have no right to do so? But the evil does not stop here. Do you think nothing of the ruin and the miseries in which so many other individuals, still remaining in Africa, are involved in consequence of carrying off so many myriads of people? Do you think nothing of their families left behind? of the connections broken? of the friendships, attachments, and relationships that are burst asunder? Do you think nothing of the miseries in consequence that are felt from generation to generation? of the privation of that happiness which might be communicated to them by the introduction of civilisation, and of mental and moral improvement?—a happiness which you with-hold from them so long as you permit the slave trade to continue.

Thus, Sir, has the perversion of British commerce carried misery instead of happiness to one whole quarter of the globe. False to the very principles of trade, misguided in our policy, and unmindful of our duty, what astonishing mischief have we brought upon that continent! If, knowing the miseries we have caused, we refuse to put a stop to them, how greatly aggravated will be the guilt of this country! Shall we then delay rendering this justice to Africa? I am sure the immediate abolition of the slave trade is the first, the principal, the most indispensable act of policy, of duty, and of justice, that the legislature of this country has to take, if it is indeed their wish to secure those important objects to which I have alluded, and which we are bound to pursue by the most solemn obligations. There is, however, one argument set up as a universal answer to every thing that can be urged on our side. The slave trade system, it is supposed, has taken such deep root in Africa, that it is absurd to think of its being eradicated; and the abolition of that share of trade carried on by Great Britain is likely to be of very little service. You are not sure, it is said, that other nations will give up the trade if you should renounce it. I answer, if this trade is as criminal as it is asserted to be, God forbid that we should hesitate in relinquishing so iniquitous a traffic; even though it should be retained by other countries! I tremble at the thought of gentlemen indulging themselves in the argument which I am combating. "We are friends," say they, "to humanity. We are second to none of you in our zeal for the good of Africa—but the French will not abolish —the Dutch will not abolish. We wait, therefore, on prudential principles, till they join us, or set us an example." How, Sir, is this enormous evil ever to be eradicated, if every nation is thus prudentially to wait till the concurrence of all the world shall have been obtained? Let me remark, too, that there is no nation in Europe that has, on the one hand, plunged so deeply into this guilt as Great Britain; or that is so likely, on the other, to be looked up to as an example. But does not this argument apply a thousand times more strongly in a contrary way? How much more justly may other nations point to us, and say, "Why should we abolish the slave trade when Great Britain has not abolished it? Britain, free as she is, just and honourable as she is, and deeply involved as she is in this commerce above all nations, not only has not abolished, but has refused to abolish." This, Sir, is the argument with which we furnish the other nations of Europe, if we again refuse to put an end to the slave trade. Instead, therefore, of imagining that by choosing to presume on their continuing it, we shall have exempted ourselves from guilt, and have transferred the whole criminality to them; let us rather reflect, that on the very principle urged against us, we shall henceforth have to answer for their crimes, as well as our own.

It has also been urged, that there is something in the disposition and nature of the Africans themselves which renders all prospect of civilisation on that continent extremely unpromising. "It has been known," says Mr. Frazer, in his evidence, "that a boy has been put to death who was refused to be purchased as a slave." This single story was deemed by that gentleman a sufficient proof of the barbarity of the Africans, and of the inutility of abolishing the slave trade. My hon. friend, however, has told you that this boy had previously run away from his master three times; that the master had to pay his value, according to the custom of his country, every time he was brought back; and that, partly from anger at the boy for running away so frequently, and partly to prevent a repetition of the same expense, he determined to put him to death. This, Sir, is the signal instance that has been dwelt upon of African barbarity. This African, we admit, was unenlightened, and altogether barbarous: but let us now ask what would a civilised and enlightened West Indian, or a body of West Indians, have done in any case of a parallel nature? I will quote you, Sir, a law passed in the West Indies in 1722; by which law this same crime of running away is, by the legislature of this island, punished with death, in the very first instance. I hope, therefore, we shall hear no more of the moral impossibility of civilising the Africans, nor have our understandings again insulted by being called upon to sanction the trade until other nations shall have set the example of abolishing it. While we have been deliberating, one nation, Denmark, not by any means remarkable for the boldness of its councils, has determined on a gradual abolition. France, it is said, will take up the trade if we relinquish it. What! Is it supposed that, in the present situation of St. Domingo, an island which used to take three-fourths of all the slaves required by the colonies of France, she, of all countries, will think of taking it up? Of the countries which remain, Portugal, Holland, and Spain—let me declare it is my opinion, that if they see us renounce the trade, they will not be disposed, even on principles of policy, to rush further into it. But I say more. How are they to furnish the capital necessary for carrying it on? If there is any aggravation of our guilt in this wretched business, it is that we have stooped to be the carriers of these miserable beings from Africa to the West Indies, for all the other powers of Europe. And if we retire from the trade, where is the fund equal to the purchase of 30,000 or 40,000 slaves?—a fund which, if we rate the slaves at £40 or £50 each, cannot require a capital of less than a million and a half, or two millions of money.

Having detained the House so long, all that I will further add shall relate to that important subject, the civilisation of Africa. Grieved am I to think that there should be a single person in this country who can look on the present uncivilised state of that continent as a ground for continuing the slave trade,—as a ground not only for refusing to attempt the improvement of Africa, but even for intercepting every ray of light which might otherwise break in upon her. Here, as in every other branch of this extensive question, the argument of our adversaries pleads against them; for surely, Sir, the present deplorable state of Africa, especially when we reflect that her chief calamities are to be ascribed to us, calls for our generous aid, rather than justifies any despair on our part of her recovery, and still less any further repetition of our injuries. I will not much longer fatigue the attention of the House; but this point has impressed itself so deeply on my mind, that I must trouble the committee with a few additional observations. Are we justified, I ask, on any one ground of theory, or by any one instance to be found in the history of the world from its very beginning to this day, in forming the supposition which I am now combating? Are we justified in supposing that the particular practice which we encourage in Africa, of men selling each other for slaves, is any symptom of a barbarism that is incurable? Are we justified in supposing that even the practice of offering up human sacrifices proves a total incapacity for civilisation? I believe it will be found that both the trade in slaves, and the still more savage custom of offering up human sacrifices, obtained in former periods throughout many of those nations which now, by the blessings of providence, and by a long progression of improvements, are advanced the farthest in civilisation. I believe that, if we reflect an instant, we shall find that this observation comes directly home to ourselves; and that, on the same ground on which we are now disposed to proscribe Africa for ever from all possibility of improvement, we might, in like manner, have been proscribed and for ever shut out from all the blessings which we now enjoy. There was a time, Sir, when even human sacrifices are said to have been offered in this island. But I would peculiarly observe on this day, for it is a case precisely in point, that the very practice of the slave trade once prevailed among us. Slaves, as we may read in Henry's *History of Great Britain,* were formerly an established article of our exports. "Great numbers," he says, "were exported like cattle, from the British coast, and were to be seen exposed for sale in the Roman market." It does not distinctly appear by what means they were procured; but there is unquestionably no small resemblance, in this particular point, between the case of our ancestors and that of the present wretched natives of Africa; for the historian tells you that "adultery, witchcraft, and debt were probably some of the chief sources of supplying the Roman market with British slaves; that prisoners taken in war were added to the number; and that there might be among them some unfortunate gamesters who, after having lost all their goods, at length staked themselves, their wives, and their children." Every one of these sources of slavery has been stated to be at this hour a source of slavery in Africa. And these circumstances, Sir, with a solitary instance or two of human sacrifices, furnish the alleged proofs that Africa labours under a natural incapacity for civilisation; that it is enthusiasm and fanaticism to think that she can ever enjoy the knowledge and the morals of Europe; that Providence never intended her to rise above a state of barbarism; that Providence has irrevocably doomed her to be only a nursery for slaves, for us free and civilised Europeans. Allow of this principle, as applied to Africa, and I should be glad to know why it might not also have been applied to ancient and uncivilised Britain. Why might not some Roman senator, reasoning on the

principles of some hon. gentlemen, and pointing to British barbarians, have predicted with equal boldness, "There is a people
that will never rise to civilisation; there is a people destined never
to be free; a people without the understanding necessary for the
attainment of useful arts; depressed by the hand of nature below
the level of the human species; and created to form a supply of
slaves for the rest of the world." Might not this have been said
in all respects as fairly and as truly of Britain herself, at that period
of her history, as it can now be said by us of the inhabitants of
Africa? We, Sir, have long since emerged from barbarism; we have
almost forgotten that we were once barbarians; we are now raised to
a situation which exhibits a striking contrast to every circumstance
by which a Roman might have characterised us, and by which we
now characterise Africa. There is, indeed, one thing wanting to
complete the contrast, and to clear us altogether from the imputa-
tion of acting even to this hour as barbarians; for we continue to
this hour a barbarous traffic in slaves; we continue it even yet,
in spite of all our great and undeniable pretensions to civilisation.
We were once as obscure among the nations of the earth, as savage
in our manners, as debased in our morals, as degraded in our
understandings, as these unhappy Africans are at present. But in
the lapse of a long series of years, by a progression slow, and for a
time almost imperceptible, we have become rich in a variety of
acquirements, favoured above measure in the gifts of Providence,
unrivalled in commerce, pre-eminent in arts, foremost in the pursuits of philosophy and science, and established in all the blessings
of civil society: we are in the possession of peace, of happiness, and
of liberty; we are under the guidance of a mild and beneficent religion; and we are protected by impartial laws, and the purest administration of justice; we are living under a system of government
which our own happy experience leads us to pronounce the best
and wisest which has ever yet been framed—a system which has
become the admiration of the world. From all these blessings we
must for ever have been shut out, had there been any truth in those
principles which some gentlemen have not hesitated to lay down
as applicable to the case of Africa. Had those principles been true,
we ourselves had languished to this hour in that miserable state
of ignorance, brutality, and degradation in which history proves

our ancestors to have been immersed. Had other nations adopted these principles in their conduct towards us; had other nations applied to Great Britain the reasoning which some of the senators of this very island now apply to Africa, ages might have passed without our emerging from barbarism; and we, who are enjoying the blessings of a British civilisation, of British laws, and British liberty, might, at this hour, have been little superior, either in morals, in knowledge, or refinement, to the rude inhabitants of the coast of Guinea.

If, then, we feel that this perpetual confinement in the fetters of brutal ignorance would have been the greatest calamity which could have befallen us; if we view with gratitude and exultation the contrast between the peculiar blessings we enjoy, and the wretchedness of the ancient inhabitants of Britain; if we shudder to think of the misery which would still have overwhelmed us had Great Britain continued to be the mart for slaves to the more civilised nations of the world, God forbid that we should any longer subject Africa to the same dreadful scourge, and preclude the light of knowledge, which has reached every other quarter of the globe from having access to her coasts! I trust we shall no longer continue this commerce, to the destruction of every improvement on that wide continent; and shall not consider ourselves as conferring too great a boon in restoring its inhabitants to the rank of human beings. I trust we shall not think ourselves too liberal if, by abolishing the slave trade, we give them of the same common chance of civilisation with other parts of the world, and that we shall now allow to Africa the opportunity—the hope—the prospect of attaining to the same blessings which we ourselves, through the favourable dispensations of Divine Providence, have been permitted, at a much more early period, to enjoy. If we listen to the voice of reason and duty, and pursue this night the line of conduct which they prescribe, some of us may live to see a reverse of that picture from which we now turn our eyes with shame and regret. We may live to behold the natives of Africa engaged in the calm occupations of industry, in the pursuits of a just and legitimate commerce. We may behold the beams of science and philosophy breaking in upon their land, which, at some happy period in still later times, may blaze with full lustre; and, joining their influence to that of pure religion, may illuminate and invigorate the most distant extremities of that immense continent. Then may we hope that even Africa, though last of all the quarters of the globe, shall enjoy at length, in the evening of her days, those blessings which have descended so plentifully upon us in a much earlier period of the world. Then also will Europe, participating in her improvement and prosperity, receive an ample recompense for the tardy kindness (if kindness it can be called) of no longer hindering that continent from extricating herself out of the darkness which, in other more fortunate regions, has been so much more speedily dispelled—

—Nos primus equis oriens afflavit anhelis;
Illic sera rubens accendit lumina Vesper.

[and when the Rising Sun has first blown upon us with his panting horses, there the red Evening Star is lighting his late fires.]
[Vergil, *Georgics* I.250-51]

Then, Sir, may be applied to Africa those words, originally used indeed with a different view—

His demum exactis • • • • •
Devenere locos laetos, et amoena vireta
Fortunatorum nemorum, sedesque beatas:
Largior hic campos Æther, et limine vestit
Purpureo.

[When at last these tasks had been performed, and the offering of the goddess had been completed, they came to joyous regions and the pleasant lawns of the happy groves and the blessed realms. Here the bright air clothes the plains more abundantly and with a radiant light, and they know their own sun, their own stars.]
[Vergil, *Aeneid* VI.637-41]

It is in this view, Sir,—it is as an atonement for our long and cruel injustice towards Africa, that the measure proposed by my hon. friend most forcibly recommends itself to my mind. The great and happy change to be expected in the state of her inhabitants is, of all the various and important benefits of the abolition, in my estimation, incomparably the most extensive and important. I shall vote, Sir, against the adjournment; and I shall also oppose to the utmost every proposition which in any way may tend either to prevent, or even to postpone for an hour, the total abolition of the slave trade; a measure which, on all the various grounds which I have stated, we are bound, by the most pressing and indispensable duty, to adopt.

Two

THE ASSERTORS
OF LIBERTY

Percy Bysshe Shelley

Percy Bysshe Shelley (1792-1822), Romantic poet, was very early associated with liberal causes. While a student at Oxford he published the *Necessity of Atheism;* for his advocacy of what was then a taboo belief he was expelled from the university. He was a great friend of the poets of the Romantic School and was also intimate with such liberals as William Godwin and Leigh Hunt. In 1819 he went to live in Italy and remained there until his death by drowning in 1822. *An Ode: To the Assertors of Liberty** was inspired by his hatred of tyranny. Although written to praise Spanish patriots, the poem was taken by many to commemorate the Peterloo Massacre. Here a crowd meeting to protest various arbitrary acts of the government was fired upon by troops summoned by the magistrates to disperse them. Although several people were killed and a number injured, the magistrates were exonerated, and the government passed the Six Acts which severely curtailed public freedom. Shelley's poem really expresses the feelings that the news of the massacre aroused in people; it is not great poetry but it contains fine liberal sentiment. "The Assertors of Liberty, Poems written in 1819," *The Poetical Works of Percy Bysshe Shelley* (Edward Moxon, London, 1840).

* In the editions of Shelley's poetry edited by Mrs. Shelley the poem bears the title given here. Hence, it is reasonable to understand, considering the date of its composition, why liberals thought it applied to the Peterloo Massacre of August 16, 1819. However, in the Oxford edition of Shelley's poetry published in 1904 a new title was appended which was as follows: "An Ode: Written 1819 Before the Spaniards had recovered their liberty." This title is based on later researches and is correct undoubtedly, but as it was not known in the nineteenth century generally, people used the earlier title and applied it to England. [Ed. note.]

An Ode: To the Assertors of Liberty

Arise, arise, arise!
There is blood on the earth that denies ye bread;
Be your wounds like eyes
To weep for the dead, the dead, the dead.
What other grief were it just to pay?
Your sons, your wives, your brethren were they;
Who said they were slain on the battle day?

Awaken, awaken, awaken!
The slave and the tyrant are twin-born foes;
Be the cold chains shaken
To the dust where your kindred repose, repose:
Their bones in the grave will start and move,
When they hear the voices of those they love,
Most loud in the holy combat above.

Wave, wave high the banner!
When Freedom is riding to conquest by:
Though the slaves that fan her
Be Famine and Toil, giving sigh for sigh.
And ye who attend her imperial car,
Lift not your hands in the banded war,
But in her defence whose children ye are.

Glory, glory, glory,
To those who have greatly suffered and done!
Never name in story
Was greater than that which ye shall have won.
Conquerors have conquered their foes alone,
Whose revenge, pride, and power they have overthrown:
Ride ye, more victorious, over your own.

Bind, bind, every brow
With crownals of violet, ivy and pine:
Hide the blood-stains now
With hues which sweet nature has made divine:
Green strength, azure hope, and eternity:
But let not the pansy among them be;
Ye were injured, and that means memory.

Three

 A PLEA FOR
CATHOLIC EMANCIPATION

Sydney Smith

Sydney Smith (1771-1845), Anglican clergyman and an ardent Whig, was a founder of the *Edinburgh Review* which was established to counter the influence of the Tory *Quarterly Review*. Sydney Smith was famous for his wit and brilliant conversation. In 1807 he published his *Plymley Letters* advocating the repeal of the laws against the Roman Catholics; he was one of the very few Anglican clergymen who were willing to tolerate on an equal basis religious bodies that differed with the Anglican Church. He was concerned for human welfare and forbearance and as he himself said to his fellow clerics on April 11, 1825, *"That no man should be subjected to civil incapacities on account of religious opinions."* Roman Catholic emancipation was finally achieved; ironically, it was brought about chiefly through the efforts of the Duke of Wellington, the darling of the country clerics and the arch-Tories. "Catholic Claims, A Speech at a meeting of the Clergy of the Archdeaconry of Yorkshire, held at Beverley in that Riding, On Monday April 11, 1825, for the purpose of Petitioning Parliament," * *The Works of the Rev. Sydney Smith* (Boston, Phillips Sampson & Co., 1857).

MR. ARCHDEACON,—It is very disagreeable to me to differ from so many worthy and respectable clergymen here assembled, and not only to differ from them, but, I am afraid, to stand

---

* I was left at this meeting in a minority of one. A poor clergyman whispered to me, that he was quite of my way of thinking, but had nine children. I begged he would remain a Protestant. [Note appended to original title.]

40

alone among them. I would much rather vote in majorities, and join in this, or any other political chorus, than to stand unassisted and alone, as I am now doing. I dislike such meetings for such purposes—I wish I could reconcile it to my conscience to stay away from them, and to my temperament to be silent at them; but if they are called by other, I deem it right to attend—if I attend I must say what I think. If it is unwise in us to meet in taverns to discuss political subjects, the fault is not mine, for I should never think of calling such a meeting. If the subject is trite, no blame is imputable to me: it is as dull to me to handle such subjects, as it is to you to hear them. The customary promise on the threshold of an inn is good entertainment for man and horse.—If there is any truth in any part of this sentence at the Tiger, at Beverley, our horses at this moment must certainly be in a state of much greater enjoyment than the masters who rode them.

It will be some amusement, however, to this meeting, to observe the schism which this question has occasioned in my own parish of Londesborough. My excellent and respectable curate, Mr. Milestones, alarmed at the effect of the pope upon the East Riding, has come here to oppose me, and there he stands, breathing war and vengeance on the Vatican. We had some previous conversation on this subject, and, in imitation of our superiors, we agreed not to make it a cabinet question.—Mr. Milestones, indeed, with that delicacy and propriety which belong to his character, expressed some scruples upon the propriety of voting against his rector, but I insisted he should come and vote against me. I assured him nothing would give me more pain than to think I had prevented, in any man, the free assertion of honest opinions. That such conduct, on his part, instead of causing jealousy and animosity between us, could not, and would not fail to increase my regard and respect for him.

I beg leave, sir, before I proceed on this subject, to state what I mean by Catholic emancipation.* I mean eligibility of Catholics to

---

* In 1673 Parliament passed the Test Act, which required all persons holding office to take the oaths of allegiance and supremacy, deny transubstantiation, and take the sacrament of the Church of England. This act made it impossible for any Roman Catholic to hold any political or military office in the state. In the late eighteenth century there was an unsuccessful move to repeal the Test Act. English sentiment remained anti-Roman Catholic as was evidenced in the

all civil offices, with the usual exceptions introduced into all bills
—jealous safeguards for the preservation of the Protestant church,
and for the regulation of the intercourse with Rome—and, lastly,
provision for the Catholic clergy.

I object, sir, to the law as it stands at present, because it is impolitic, and because it is unjust. It is impolitic, because it exposes
this country to the greatest danger in time of war. Can you believe,
sir, can any man of the most ordinary turn for observation, believe,
that the monarchs of Europe mean to leave this country in the quiet
possession of the high station which it at present holds? Is it not
obvious that a war is coming on between the governments of law
and the governments of despotism?—that the weak and tottering
race of the Bourbons will (whatever our wishes may be) be compelled
to gratify the wounded vanity of the French, by plunging them into
a war with England. Already they are pitying the Irish people, as
you pity the West Indian slaves—already they are opening colleges
for the reception of Irish priests. Will they wait for your tardy wisdom and reluctant liberality? Is not the present state of Ireland a
premium upon early invasion? Does it not hold out the most allur-
ing invitation to your enemies to begin? And if the flag of any
hostile power in Europe is unfurled in that unhappy country, is
there one Irish peasant who will not hasten to join it?—and not only
the peasantry, sir; the peasantry begin these things, but the peasantry do not end them—they are soon joined by an order a little
above them—and then, after a trifling success, a still superior class
think it worth while to try the risk: men are hurried into a rebellion, as the oxen are pulled into the cave of Cacus—tail foremost.
The mob first, who have nothing to lose but their lives, of which
every Irishman has nine—then comes the shopkeeper—then the
parish priest—then the vicar-general—then Dr. Doyle, and, lastly,
Daniel O'Connell. But if the French were to make the same blunders

---

"Gordon Riots" of 1780. William Pitt intended to join Roman Catholic emancipation with the Irish union but George III would not allow it, and consequently the Irish union was never really accepted by the mass of the Irish. By
1820 most reasonable people in England favored Catholic Emancipation, but
the die-hard Tories and King George IV did not. Finally, on May 9, 1829, the
Test Act was repealed as well as the remaining recusancy legislation, and Roman
Catholics were given political equality with their Protestant fellow citizens.
[Ed. note.]

respecting Ireland as Napoleon committed, if wind and weather preserved Ireland for you a second time, still all your resources would be crippled by watching Ireland. The force employed for this might liberate Spain and Portugal, protect India, or accomplish any great purpose of offence or defence.

War, sir, seems to be almost as natural a state to mankind as peace; but if you could hope to escape war, is there a more powerful receipt for destroying the prosperity of any country than these eternal jealousies and distinctions between the two religions? What man will carry his industry and his capital into a country where his yard measure is a sword, his pounce-box a powder-flask, and his ledger a return of killed and wounded? Where a cat will get, there I know a cotton-spinner will penetrate; but let these gentlemen wait till a few of their factories have been burnt down, till one or two respectable merchants of Manchester have been carded, and till they have seen the cravatists hanging the shanavists in cotton twist. In the present fervour for spinning, ourang-outangs, sir, would be employed to spin, if they could be found in sufficient quantities; but miserably will those reasoners be disappointed who repose upon cotton—not upon justice—and who imagine this great question can be put aside, because a few hundred Irish spinners are gaining a morsel of bread by the overflowing industry of the English market.

But what right have you to continue these rules, sir, these laws of exclusion? What necessity can you show for it? Is the reigning monarch a concealed Catholic?—Is his successor an open one?—Is there a disputed succession?—Is there a Catholic pretender? If some of these circumstances are said to have justified the introduction, and others the continuation of these measures, why does not the disappearance of all these circumstances justify the repeal of the restrictions? If you must be unjust—if it is a luxury you cannot live without—reserve your injustice for the weak, and not for the strong —persecute the Unitarians, muzzle the Ranters, be unjust to a few thousand sectaries, not to six millions—galvanize a frog, don't galvanize a tiger.

If you go into a parsonage house in the country, Mr. Archdeacon, you see sometimes a style and fashion of furniture which does very well for us, but which has had its day in London. It is seen in London no more; it is banished to the provinces; from the gentlemen's houses of the provinces these pieces of furniture, as soon as they are discovered to be unfashionable, descend to the farm-houses, then to cottages, then to the faggot-heap, then to the dunghill. As it is with furniture, so is it with arguments. I hear at country meetings many arguments against the Catholics which are never heard in London; their London existence is over—they are only to be met with in the provinces, and there they are fast hastening down, with clumsy chairs and ill-fashioned sofas, to another order of men. But, sir, as they are not yet gone where I am sure they are going, I shall endeavour to point out their defects, and to accelerate their descent.

Many gentlemen now assembled at the Tiger Inn, at Beverley, believe that the Catholics do not keep faith with heretics; these gentlemen ought to know that Mr. Pitt put this very question to six of the leading Catholic universities in Europe. He inquired of them whether this tenet did or did not constitute any part of the Catholic faith. The question received from these universities the most decided negative; they denied that such doctrine formed any part of the creed of Catholics. Such doctrine, sir, is denied upon oath, in the bill now pending in Parliament, a copy of which I hold in my hand. The denial of such a doctrine upon oath is the only means by which a Catholic can relieve himself from his present incapacities. If a Catholic, therefore, sir, will not take the oath, he is not relieved, and remains where you wish him to remain; if he does take the oath, you are safe from his peril: if he has no scruple about oaths, of what consequence is it whether this bill passes, the very object of which is to relieve him from oaths? Look at the fact, sir. Do the Protestant cantons of Switzerland, living under the same state with the Catholic cantons, complain that no faith is kept with heretics? Do not the Catholics and Protestants in the kingdom of the Netherlands meet in one common Parliament? Could they pursue a common purpose, have common friends, and common enemies, if there was a shadow of truth in this doctrine imputed to the Catholics? The religious affairs of this last kingdom are managed with the strictest impartiality to both sects? ten Catholics and ten Protestants (gentlemen need not look so much surprised to hear it), positively meet together, sir, in the same room. They constitute what is called the religious committee for the kingdom of the Netherlands, and so extremely desirous are they of preserving the strictest impartiality, that they have chosen a Jew for their secretary. Their conduct has been unimpeachable and unimpeached; the two sects are at peace with each other; and the doctrine, that no faith is kept with heretics, would, I assure you, be very little credited at Amsterdam or the Hague, cities as essentially Protestant as the town of Beverley.

Wretched is our condition, and still more wretched the condition of Ireland, if the Catholic does not respect his oath. He serves on grand and petty juries in both countries; we trust our lives, our liberties, and our properties, to his conscientious reverence of an oath, and yet, when it suits the purposes of party to bring forth this argument, we say he has no respect for oaths. The right to a landed estate of 3000£. per annum was decided last week, in York, by a jury, the foreman of which was a Catholic; does any human being, harbour a thought, that this gentleman, whom we all know and respect, would, under any circumstances, have thought more lightly of the obligation of an oath, than his Protestant brethren of the box? We all disbelieve these arguments of Mr. A. the Catholic, and of Mr. B. the Catholic: but we believe them of Catholics in general, of the abstract Catholics, of the Catholic of the Tiger Inn, at Beverley, the formidable unknown Catholic, that is so apt to haunt our clerical meetings.

I observe that some gentlemen who argue this question, are very bold about other offices, but very jealous lest Catholic gentlemen should become justices of the peace. If this jealousy is justifiable anywhere, it is justifiable in Ireland, where some of the best and most respectable magistrates are Catholics.

It is not true that the Roman Catholic religion is what it was. I meet that assertion with a plump denial. The pope does not dethrone kings, nor give away kingdoms, does not extort money, has given up, in some instances, the nomination of bishops to Catholic princes, in some, I believe, to Protestant princes; Protestant worship is now carried on at Rome. In the Low Countries, the seat of the Duke of Alva's cruelties, the Catholic tolerates the Protestant, and sits with him in the same Parliament—the same in Hungary —the same in France. The first use which even the Spanish people made of their ephemeral liberty, was to destroy the Inquisition. It was destroyed also by the mob of Portugal. I am so far from thinking the Catholic not to be more tolerant than he was, that I am much afraid the English, who gave the first lesson of toleration to mankind, will very soon have a great deal to learn from their pupils.

Some men quarrel with the Catholics, because their language was violent in the Association; but a groan or two, sir, after two hundred years of incessant tyranny, may surely be forgiven. A few warm phrases to compensate the legal massacre of a million of Irishmen are not unworthy of our pardon. All this hardly deserves the eternal incapacity of holding civil offices. Then they quarrel with the Bible Society; in other words they vindicate that ancient tenet of their church, that the Scriptures are not to be left to the unguided judgment of the laity. The objection to Catholics is, that they did what Catholics ought to do—and do not many prelates of our church object to the Bible Society, and contend that the Scriptures ought not to be circulated without the comment of the Prayer Book and the Articles? If they are right, the Catholics are not wrong; and if the Catholics are wrong, they are in such good company, that we ought to respect their errors.

Why not pay their clergy? the Presbyterian clergy in the north of Ireland are paid by the state: the Catholic clergy of Canada are provided for: the priests of the Hindoos are, I believe, in some of their temples, paid by the Company. You must surely admit that the Catholic religion (the religion of two-thirds of Europe) is better than no religion. I do not regret that the Irish are under the dominion of the priests. I am glad that so savage a people as the lower orders of Irish are under the dominion of their priests; for it is a step gained to place such beings under any influence, and the clergy are always the first civilizers of mankind. The Irish are deserted by their natural aristocracy, and I should wish to make their priesthood respectable in their appearance, and easy in their circumstances. A government provision has produced the most important changes in the opinions of the Presbyterian clergy of the north of Ireland, and has changed them from levellers and Jacobins into reasonable men; it would not fail to improve most materially the political opinions of the Catholic priests. This cannot, however, be done, without the emancipation of the laity. No priest would dare to accept a salary from government, unless this preliminary was settled. I am aware it would give to government a tremendous power in that country; but I must choose the least of two evils. The great point, as physicians say, in some diseases, is to resist the tendency to death. The great object of our day is to prevent the loss of Ireland, and the consequent ruin of England; to obviate the tendency to death; we will first keep the patient alive, and then dispute about his diet and his medicine.

Suppose a law were passed, that no clergyman who had ever held a living in the East Riding, could be made a bishop. Many gentlemen here (who have no hopes of ever being removed from their parishes) would feel the restriction of the law as a considerable degradation. We should soon be pointed at as a lower order of clergymen. It would not be long before the common people would find some fortunate epithet for us, and it would not be long either before we should observe in our brethren of the north and west an air of superiority, which would aggravate not a little the justice of the privation. Every man feels the insult thrown upon his *caste;* the insulted party falls lower, every body else becomes higher. There are heart-burnings and recollections. Peace flies from that land. The volume of parliamentary evidence I have brought here is loaded with the testimony of witnesses of all ranks and occupations, stating to the House of Commons the undoubted effects produced upon the lower order of Catholics by these disqualifying laws, and the lively interest they take in their removal. I have seventeen quotations, sir, from this evidence, and am ready to give any gentleman my references; but I forbear to read them, from compassion to my reverend brethren, who have trotted many miles to vote against the pope, and who will trot back in the dark, if I attempt to throw additional light upon the subject.

I have also, sir, a high-spirited class of gentlemen to deal with, who will do nothing from fear, who admit the danger, but think it disgraceful to act as if they feared it. There is a degree of fear, which destroys a man's faculties, renders him incapable of acting, and makes him ridiculous. There is another sort of fear, which enables a man to foresee a coming evil, to measure it, to examine his powers of resistance, to balance the evil of submission against the evils of opposition or defeat, and if he thinks he must be ultimately overpowered, leads him to find a good escape in a good time. I can see no possible disgrace in feeling this sort of fear, and in listening to its suggestions. But it is mere cant to say that men will not be actuated by fear in such questions as these. Those who pretend not to fear now would be the first to fear upon the approach of danger; it is always the case with this distant valour. Most of the concessions which have been given to the Irish have been given to fear. Ireland would have been lost to this country, if the British legislature had not, with all the rapidity and precipitation of the truest panic, passed those acts which Ireland did not ask, but demanded in the time of her armed associations. I should not think a man brave, but mad, who did not fear the treasons and rebellions of Ireland in time of war. I should think him not dastardly, but consummately wise, who provided against them in time of peace. The Catholic question has made a greater progress since the opening of this Parliament than I ever remember it to have made, and it has made that progress from fear alone. The House of Commons were astonished by the union of the Irish Catholics. They saw that Catholic Ireland had discovered her strength, and stretched out her limbs, and felt manly powers, and called for manly treatment; and the House of Commons wisely and practically yielded to the innovations of time, and the shifting attitude of human affairs.

I admit the church, sir, to be in great danger. I am sure the state is so also. My remedy for these evils is, to enter into an alliance with the Irish people—to conciliate the clergy, by giving them pensions —to loyalize the laity, by putting them on a footing with the Protestant. My remedy is the old one, approved of from the beginning of the world, to lessen dangers, by increasing friends, and appeasing enemies. I think it most probable, that under this system of crown patronage, the clergy will be quiet. A Catholic layman, who finds all the honours of the state open to him, will not, I think, run into treason and rebellion—will not live with a rope about his neck, in order to turn our bishops out, and put his own in; he may not, too, be of opinion that the utility of his bishop will be four times as great, because his income is four times as large; but whether he is or not, he will never endanger his sweet acres (large measure) for such questions as these. Anti-Trinitarian Dissenters sit in the House of Commons, whom we believe to be condemned to the punishments of another world. There is no limit to the introduction of Dissenters into both houses—Dissenting Lords or Dissenting Commons. What mischief have Dissenters for this last century and a half plotted against the Church of England? The Catholic lord and the Catholic gentleman (restored to their fair rights) will never join with levellers and Iconoclasts. You will find them defending you hereafter against your Protestant enemies.—The crosier in any hand, the mitre on any head, are more tolerable in the eyes of a Catholic than doxological Barebones and tonsured Cromwell.

We preach to our congregations, sir, that a tree is known by its fruits. By the fruits it produces I will judge your system. What has it done for Ireland? New Zealand is emerging—Otaheite is emerging —Ireland is not emerging—she is still veiled in darkness—her children, safe under no law, live in the very shadow of death. Has your system of exclusion made Ireland rich? Has it made Ireland loyal? Has it made Ireland free? Has it made Ireland happy? How is the wealth of Ireland proved? Is it by the naked, idle, suffering savages, who are slumbering on the mud floor of their cabins? In what does the loyalty of Ireland consist? Is it in the eagerness with which they would range themselves under the hostile banner of any invader, for your destruction and for your distress? Is it liberty when men breathe and move among the bayonets of English soldiers? Is their happiness and their history any thing but such a tissue of murders, burnings, hanging, famine, and disease, as never existed before in the annals of the world?—This is the system which, I am sure, with very different intentions, and different views of its effects, you are met this day to uphold. These are the dreadful consequences, which those laws your petition prays may be continued, have produced upon Ireland. From the principles of that system, from the cruelty of those laws, I turn, and turn with the homage of my whole heart, to that memorable proclamation which the head of our church— the present monarch of these realms—has lately made to his hereditary dominions of Hanover—*That no man should be subjected to civil incapacities on account of religious opinions.* Sir, there have been many memorable things done in this reign. Hostile armies have been destroyed; fleets have been captured; formidable combinations have been broken to pieces—*but this sentiment, in the mouth of a king,* deserves more than all glories and victories the notice of that historian who is destined to tell to future ages the deeds of the English people. I hope he will lavish upon it every gem which glitters in the cabinet of genius, and so uphold it to the world that it will be remembered when Waterloo is forgotten, and when the fall of Paris is blotted out from the memory of man. Great as it is, sir, this is not the only pleasure I have received in these latter days. I have seen, within these few weeks, a degree of wisdom in our mercantile laws, such superiority to vulgar prejudice, views so just and so profound, that it seemed to me as if I was reading the works of a speculative economist, rather than the improvement of a practical politician, agreed to by a legislative assembly, and upon the eve of being carried into execution, for the benefit of a great people. Let who will be their master, I honour and praise the ministers who have learnt such a lesson. I rejoice that I have lived to see such an improvement in English affairs—that the stubborn resistance to all improvement —the contempt of all scientific reasoning, and the rigid adhesion to every stupid error which so long characterized the proceedings of this country, are fast giving away to better things, under better men, placed in better circumstances.

I confess it is not without severe pain that, in the midst of all this expansion and improvement, I perceive that in our profession we are still calling for the same exclusion—still asking that the same fetters may be riveted on our fellow-creatures—still mistaking what constitutes the weakness and misfortune of the church, for that which contributes to its glory, its dignity, and its strength. Sir, there are two petitions at this moment in this house, against two of the wisest and best measures which ever came into the British Parliament, against the impending corn law and against the Catholic emancipation—the one bill intended to increase the comforts, and the other to allay the bad passions of man.—Sir, I am not in a situation of life to do much good, but I will take care that I will not willingly do any evil.—The wealth of the Riding should not tempt me to petition against either of those bills. With the corn bill, I have nothing to do at this time. Of the Catholic emancipation bill, I shall say, that it will be the foundation stone of a lasting religious peace; that it will give to Ireland not all that it wants, but what it most wants, and without which no other boon will be of any avail.

When this bill passes, it will be a signal to all the religious sects of that unhappy country to lay aside their mutual hatred, and to live in peace, as equal men should live under equal law—when this bill passes, the Orange flag of the rebel will fall—when this bill passes, no other flag will fly in the land of Erin than that flag which blends the lion with the harp—that flag which, wherever it does fly, is the sign of freedom and of joy—the only banner in Europe which floats over a limited king and a free people.

Four

PARLIAMENTARY
REFORM

Thomas Babington Macaulay

Thomas Babington Macaulay, first Baron Macaulay (1800-1859), historian, barrister, and reformer, was a Whig M.P. and sat for the borough of Calne. From 1834 to 1838 he was a member of the supreme council of India where he practically single-handedly created India's entire educational system. He wrote much, he was a constant contributor to the *Edinburgh Review,* and he is particularly remembered for his *History of England.* With Brougham, Bentham, and Mill, Macaulay can be considered one of the seminal minds of the nineteenth century. On March 1, 1832, Lord John Russell introduced the great Reform Bill; Russell's speech was the prologue for the long parliamentary debate which followed. On the second night Macaulay delivered the speech given here. Macaulay's speech—his initial effort in the Commons—had a tremendous impact on both sides of the House. It expressed the Whig views on the whole concept of reform and summarized the philosophy of the essential need for change of the constitution. Indeed, this speech is probably the best exposition of the constitutional reforming tradition. "Parliamentary Reform, The House of Commons, 2 March, 1831," *Speeches of Lord Macaulay* (London, Longmans Green & Co., 1875).

It is a circumstance, Sir, of happy augury for the motion before the House, that almost all those who have opposed it have declared themselves hostile on principle to Parliamentary Reform. Two members, I think, have confessed that, . . . they disapprove

52

of the plan now submitted to us, . . . Yet even those gentlemen have used, as far as I have observed, no arguments which would not apply as strongly to the most moderate change as to that which has been proposed by His Majesty's Government. I say, Sir, that I consider this as a circumstance of happy augury. For what I feared was, not the opposition of those who are averse to all Reform, but the disunion of reformers. I knew that, during three months, every reformer had been employed in conjecturing what the plan of the Government would be. I knew that every reformer had imagined in his own mind a scheme differing doubtless in some points from that which my noble friend, the Paymaster of the Forces,* has developed. I felt, therefore, great apprehension that one person would be dissatisfied with one part of the bill, that another person would be dissatisfied with another part, and that thus our whole strength would be wasted in internal dissensions. That apprehension is now at an end. I have seen with delight the perfect concord which prevails among all who deserve the name of reformers in this House; and I trust that I may consider it as an omen of the concord which will prevail among reformers throughout the country. I will not, Sir, at present express any opinion as to the details of the bill; but, having during the last twenty-four hours given the most diligent consideration to its general principles, I have no hesitation in pronouncing it a wise, noble, and comprehensive measure, skilfully framed for the healing of great distempers, for the securing at once of the public liberties, and of the public repose, and for the reconciling and knitting together of all the orders of the State.

The hon. Baronet who has just sat down [Sir John Walsh] has told us that the Ministers have attempted to unite two inconsistent principles in one abortive measure. Those were his very words. He thinks, if I understand him rightly, that we ought either to leave the representative system such as it is,† or to make it perfectly sym-

---

* Lord John Russell who had introduced the bill. [Ed. note.]

† Before 1832 Parliament had two types of members: the knights of the shire —two members from each county elected as representatives at large with a franchise based on the forty shilling freehold; and borough members—each borough that had been granted the right to elect M.P.'s generally sent two persons, and the franchise varied from relatively democratic to extremely limited. Since the reign of Charles II there had been no basic alteration in Parliamentary representation. [Ed. note.]

metrical. I think, Sir, that the Ministers would have acted unwisely if they had taken either course. Their principle is plain, rational, and consistent. It is this, to admit the middle class to a large and direct share in the representation, without any violent shock to the institutions of our country. I understand those cheers; but surely the gentlemen who utter them will allow that the change which will be made in our institutions by this bill is far less violent than that which, according to the hon. Baronet, ought to be made if we make any Reform at all. I praise the Ministers for not attempting, at the present time, to make the representation uniform.** I praise them for not effacing the old distinction between the towns and the counties, and for not assigning Members to districts, according to the American practice, by the Rule of Three. The Government has, in my opinion, done all that was necessary for the removing of a great practical evil, and no more than was necessary.

I consider this, Sir, as a practical question. I rest my opinion on no general theory of government. I distrust all general theories of government. I will not positively say that there is any form of polity which may not, in some conceivable circumstances, be the best possible. I believe that there are societies in which every man may safely be admitted to vote. Gentlemen may jeer, but such is my opinion. I say, Sir, that there are countries in which the condition of the labouring classes is such that they may safely be intrusted with the right of electing members of the Legislature. If the labourers of England were in that state in which I, from my soul, wish to see them, if employment were always plentiful, wages always high, food always cheap, if a large family were considered not as an encumbrance but as a blessing, the principal objections to Universal Suffrage would, I think, be removed. Universal Suffrage exists in the United States without producing any very frightful consequences; and I do not believe that the people of those States, or of any part of the world, are in any good quality naturally superior to our own

** The bill when finally enacted redistributed 143 seats (this redistribution to some degree reflected the chief centers of population), established a uniform borough franchise, and retained the forty shilling requirement for the election of knights of the shire. While the new legislation doubled the total electorate, England was far from having the universal suffrage that existed at the same time in the United States. Only with the later reform acts of the nineteenth century was universal manhood suffrage attained. [Ed. note.]

countrymen. But, unhappily, the labouring classes in England, and in all old countries, are occasionally in a state of great distress. Some of the causes of this distress are, I fear, beyond the control of the Government. We know what effect distress produces, even on people more intelligent than the great body of the labouring classes can possibly be. We know that it makes even wise men irritable, unreasonable, credulous, eager for immediate relief, heedless of remote consequences. There is no quackery in medicine, religion, or politics which may not impose even on a powerful mind, when that mind has been disordered by pain or fear. It is, therefore, no reflection on the poorer class of Englishmen, who are not, and who cannot in the nature of things be, highly educated, to say that distress produces on them its natural effects, those effects which it would produce on the Americans, or on any other people, that it blinds their judgment, that it inflames their passions, that it makes them prone to believe those who flatter them, and to distrust those who would serve them. For the sake, therefore, of the whole society, for the sake of the labouring classes themselves, I hold it to be clearly expedient that, in a country like this, the right of suffrage should depend on a pecuniary qualification.

But, Sir, every argument which would induce me to oppose Universal Suffrage induces me to support the plan which is now before us. I am opposed to Universal Suffrage because I think that it would produce a destructive revolution. I support this plan because I am sure that it is our best security against a revolution. The noble Paymaster of the Forces hinted, delicately indeed and remotely, at this subject. He spoke of the danger of disappointing the expectations of the nation; and for this he was charged with threatening the House. Sir, in the year 1817, the late Lord Londonderry proposed a suspension of the Habeas Corpus Act. On that occasion he told the House that, unless the measures which he recommended were adopted, the public peace could not be preserved. Was he accused of threatening the House? Again, in the year 1819, he proposed the laws known by the name of the Six Acts. He then told the House that, unless the executive power was reinforced, all the institutions of the country would be overturned by popular violence. Was he then accused of threatening the House? Will any gentleman say that it is parliamentary and decorous to urge the danger arising from popular discontent as an argument for severity; but that it is unparliamentry and indecorous to urge that same danger as an argument for conciliation? I, Sir, do entertain great apprehension for the fate of my country. I do in my conscience believe that, unless the plan proposed, or some similar plan, be speedily adopted, great and terrible calamities will befall us. Entertaining this opinion, I think myself bound to state it, not as a threat, but as a reason. I support this bill because it will improve our institutions; but I support it also because it tends to preserve them. That we may exclude those whom it is necessary to exclude, we must admit those whom it may be safe to admit. At present we oppose the schemes of revolutionists with only one half, with only one quarter of our proper force. We say, and we say justly, that it is not by mere numbers, but by property and intelligence, that the nation ought to be governed. Yet, saying this, we exclude from all share in the government great masses of property and intelligence, great numbers of those who are most interested in preserving tranquillity, and who know best how to preserve it. We do more. We drive over to the side of revolution those whom we shut out from power. Is this a time when the cause of law and order can spare one of its natural allies?

My noble friend, the Paymaster of the Forces, happily described the effect which some parts of our representative system would produce on the mind of a foreigner, who had heard much of our freedom and greatness. If, Sir, I wished to make such a foreigner clearly understand what I consider as the great defects of our system, I would conduct him through that immense city which lies to the north of Great Russell Street and Oxford Street, a city superior in size and in population to the capitals of many mighty kingdoms; and probably superior in opulence, intelligence, and general respectability to any city in the world. I would conduct him through that interminable succession of streets and squares, all consisting of well-built and well-furnished houses. I would make him observe the brilliancy of the shops, and the crowd of well-appointed equipages. I would show him that magnificent circle of palaces which surrounds the Regent's Park. I would tell him that the rental of this district was far greater than that of the whole kingdom of Scotland at the time of the Union. And then I would tell him that this was an unrepresented district. It is needless to give any more instances.

It is needless to speak of Manchester, Birmingham, Leeds, Sheffield, with no representation, or of Edinburgh and Glasgow with a mock representation. If a property tax were now imposed on the principle that no person who had less than a hundred and fifty pounds a year should contribute, I should not be surprised to find that one-half in number and value of the contributors had no votes at all; and it would, beyond all doubt, be found that one-fiftieth part in number and value of the contributors had a larger share of the representation than the other forty-nine fiftieths. This is not government by property. It is government by certain detached portions and fragments of property, selected from the rest, and preferred to the rest, on no rational principle whatever.

To say that such a system is ancient is no defence. My hon. friend, the member for the University of Oxford [Sir Robert Harry Inglis], challenges us to show that the Constitution was ever better than it is. Sir, we are legislators, not antiquaries. The question for us is, not whether the Constitution was better formerly, but whether we can make it better now. In fact, however, the system was not in ancient times by any means so absurd as it is in our age. One noble Lord [Lord Stormont] has to-night told us that the town of Aldborough, which he represents, was not larger in the time of Edward the First than it is at present. The line of its walls, he assures us, may still be traced. It is now built up to that line. He argues, therefore, that as the founders of our representative institutions gave members to Aldborough when it was as small as it now is, those who would disfranchise it on account of its smallness have no right to say that they are recurring to the original principle of our representative institutions. But does the noble Lord remember the change which has taken place in the country during the last five centuries? Does he remember how much England has grown in population, while Aldborough has been standing still? Does he consider, that in the time of Edward the First, the kingdom did not contain two millions of inhabitants? It now contains nearly fourteen millions. A hamlet of the present day would have been a town of some importance in the time of our early Parliaments. Aldborough may be absolutely as considerable a place as ever. But compared with the kingdom, it is much less considerable, by the noble Lord's own showing, than when it first elected burgesses. My hon. friend, the

member for the University of Oxford, has collected numerous instances of the tyranny which the kings and nobles anciently exercised, both over this House and over the electors. It is not strange
that, in times when nothing was held sacred, the rights of the people,
and of the representative of the people, should not have been held
sacred. The proceedings which my hon. friend has mentioned no
more prove that by the ancient constitution of the realm this House
ought to be a tool of the king and of the aristocracy, than the Be-
nevolences and the Shipmoney prove their own legality, or than those
unjustifiable arrests which took place long after the ratification of
the great Charter and even after the Petition of Right, prove that
the subject was not anciently entitled to his personal liberty. We
talk of the wisdom of our ancestors; and in one respect at least they
were wiser than we. They legislated for their own times. They
looked at the England which was before them. They did not think
it necessary to give twice as many members to York as they gave to
London, because York had been the capital of Britain in the time
of Constantius Chlorus; and they would have been amazed indeed
if they had foreseen that a city of more than a hundred thousand
inhabitants would be left without representatives in the nineteenth
century, merely because it stood on ground which in the thirteenth
century had been occupied by a few huts. They framed a representative system, which, though not without defects and irregularities,
was well adapted to the state of England in their time. But a great
revolution took place. The character of the old corporations changed.
New forms of property came into existence. New portions of society
rose into importance. There were in our rural districts rich culti-
vators, who were not freeholders. There were in our capital rich
traders, who were not livery-men. Towns shrank into villages. Villages swelled into cities larger than the London of the Plantagenets.
Unhappily while the natural growth of society went on, the artificial
polity continued unchanged. The ancient form of the representation
remained; and precisely because the form remained, the spirit departed. Then came that pressure almost to bursting, the new wine
in the old bottles, the new society under the old institutions. It is
now time for us to pay a decent, a rational, a manly reverence to our
ancestors, not by superstitiously adhering to what they, in other
circumstances, would have done. All history is full of revolutions,

produced by causes similar to those which are now operating in England. A portion of the community which had been of no account expands and becomes strong. It demands a place in the system, suited, not to its former weakness, but to its present power. If this be granted, all is well. If this is refused, then comes the struggle between the young energy of one class and the ancient privileges of another. Such was the struggle between the Plebeians and the Patricians of Rome. Such was the struggle of the Italian allies for admission to the full rights of Roman citizens. Such was the struggle of our North American colonies against the mother country. Such was the struggle which the Third Estate of France maintained against the aristocracy of birth. Such was the struggle which the Roman Catholics of Ireland maintained against the aristocracy of creed. Such is the struggle which the free people of colour in Jamaica are now maintaining against the aristocracy of skin. Such, finally, is the struggle which the middle classes in England are maintaining against an aristocracy of mere locality, against an aristocracy the principles of which is to invest a hundred drunken potwallopers in one place, or the owner of a ruined hovel in another, with powers which are withheld from cities renowned to the farthest ends of the earth for the marvels of their wealth and of their industry.

But these great cities, says my honourable friend the member for the University of Oxford, are virtually, though not directly, represented. Are not the wishes of Manchester, he asks, as much consulted as those of any town which sends members to Parliament? Now, Sir, I do not understand how a power which is salutary when exercised virtually can be noxious when exercised directly. If the wishes of Manchester have as much weight with us as they would have under a system which should give representatives to Manchester, how can there be any danger in giving representatives to Manchester? A virtual representative is, I presume, a man who acts as a direct representative would act; for surely it would be absurd to say that a man virtually represents the people of Manchester who is in the habit of saying No, when a man directly representing the people of Manchester would say Ay. The utmost that can be expected from virtual representation is that it may be as good as direct representation. If so, why not grant direct representation to places which, as everybody allows, ought, by some process or other, to be represented?

If it be said that there is an evil in change as change, I answer that there is also an evil in discontent as discontent. This, indeed, is the strongest part of our case. It is said that the system works well. I deny it. I deny that a system works well which the people regard with aversion. We may say here that it is a good system and a perfect system. But if any man were to say so to any six hundred and fifty-eight respectable farmers or shopkeepers, chosen by lot in any part of England, he would be hooted down, and laughed to scorn. Are these the feelings with which any part of the government ought to be regarded? Above all, are these the feelings with which the popular branch of the legislature ought to be regarded? It is almost as essential to the utility of a House of Commons that it should possess the confidence of the people, as that it should deserve that confidence. Unfortunately, that which is in theory the popular part of our government, is in practice the unpopular part. Who wishes to dethrone the King? Who wishes to turn the Lords out of their House? Here and there a crazy radical, whom the boys in the street point at as he walks along. Who wishes to alter the constitution of this House? The whole people. It is natural that it should be so. The House of Commons is, in the language of Mr. Burke, a check, not on the people, but for the people. While that check is efficient, there is no reason to fear that the King or the nobles will oppress the people. But if that check requires checking, how is it to be checked? If the salt shall lose its savour, wherewith shall we season it? The distrust with which the nation regards this House may be unjust. But what then? Can you remove that distrust? That it exists cannot be denied. That it is an evil cannot be denied. That it is an increasing evil cannot be denied. One gentleman tells us that it has been produced by the late events in France and Belgium; another, that it is the effect of seditious works which have lately been published. If this feeling be of origin so recent, I have read history to little purpose. Sir, this alarming discontent is not the growth of a day or of a year. If there be any symptoms by which it is possible to distinguish the chronic diseases of the body politic from its passing inflammations, all those symptoms exist in the present case. The taint has been gradually becoming more extensive and more malignant, through the whole lifetime of two generations. We have tried anodynes. We have tried cruel operations. What are we to try now?

Who flatters himself that he can turn this feeling back? Does there remain any argument which escaped the comprehensive intellect of Mr. Burke, or the subtlety of Mr. Windham? Does there remain any species of coercion which was not tried by Mr. Pitt and by Lord Londonderry? We have had laws. We have had blood. New treasons have been created. The Press has been shackled. The Habeas Corpus Act has been suspended. Public meetings have been prohibited. The event has proved that these expedients were mere palliatives. You are at the end of your palliatives. The evil remains. It is more formidable than ever. What is to be done?

Under such circumstances, a great plan of reconciliation, prepared by the ministers of the Crown, has been brought before us in a manner which gives additional lustre to a noble name, inseparably associated during two centuries with the dearest liberties of the English people. I will not say that this plan is in all its details precisely such as I might wish it to be; but it is founded on a great and a sound principle. It takes away a vast power from a few. It distributes that power through the great mass of the middle order. Every man, therefore, who thinks as I think is bound to stand firmly by ministers who are resolved to stand or fall with this measure. Were I one of them, I would sooner, infinitely sooner, fall with such a measure than stand by any other means that ever supported a Cabinet.

My hon. friend, the member for the University of Oxford, tells us that if we pass this law England will soon be a republic. The reformed House of Commons will, according to him, before it has sat ten years, depose the King and expel the Lords from their House. Sir, if my hon. friend could prove this, he would have succeeded in bringing an argument for democracy infinitely stronger than any that is to be found in the works of Paine. My hon. friend's proposition is in fact this: that our monarchical and aristocratical institutions have no hold on the public mind of England; that these institutions are regarded with aversion by a majority of the middle class. This, Sir, I say, is plainly deducible from his proposition; for he tells us that the representatives of the middle class will inevitably abolish royalty and nobility within ten years: and there is surely no reason to think that the representatives of the middle class will be more inclined to a democratic revolution than their constituents.

Now, Sir, if I were convinced that the great body of the middle class in England look with aversion on monarchy and aristocracy, I should be forced, much against my will, to come to this conclusion, that monarchical and aristocratical institutions are unsuited to my country. Monarchy and aristocracy, valuable and useful as I think them, are still valuable and useful as means, and not as ends. The end of government is the happiness of the people; and I do not conceive that, in a country like this, the happiness of the people can be promoted by a form of government in which the middle classes place no confidence, and which exists only because the middle classes have no organ by which to make their sentiments known. But, Sir, I am fully convinced that the middle classes sincerely wish to uphold the Royal prerogatives and the constitutional rights of the Peers. What facts does my hon. friend produce in support of his opinion? One fact only; and that a fact which has absolutely nothing to do with the question. The effect of this Reform, he tells us, would be to make the House of Commons all-powerful. It was all-powerful once before, in the beginning of 1649. Then it cut off the head of the King, and abolished the House of Peers. Therefore, if it again has the supreme power, it will act in the same manner. Now, Sir, it was not the House of Commons that cut off the head of Charles the First; nor was the House of Commons then all-powerful. It had been greatly reduced in numbers by successive expulsions. It was under the absolute dominion of the army. A majority of the House was willing to take the terms offered by the King. The soldiers turned out the majority; and the minority, not a sixth part of the whole House, passed those votes of which my hon. friend speaks, votes of which the middle classes disapproved then, and of which they disapprove still.

My hon. friend, and almost all the gentlemen who have taken the same side with him in this debate, have dwelt much on the utility of close and rotten boroughs. It is by means of such boroughs, they tell us, that the ablest men have been introduced into Parliament. It is true that many distinguished persons have represented places of this description. But, Sir, we must judge of a form of government by its general tendency, not by happy accidents. Every form of government has its happy accidents. Despotism has its happy accidents. Yet we are not disposed to abolish all constitutional checks, to place an absolute master over us, and to take our chance whether he may be a Caligula or a Marcus Aurelius. In whatever way the House of Commons may be chosen, some able men will be chosen in that way who would not be chosen in any other way. If there were a law that the hundred tallest men in England should be Members of Parliament, there would probably be some able men among those who would come into the House by virtue of this law. If the hundred persons whose names stand first in the alphabetical list of the Court Guide were made Members of Parliament, there would probably be able men among them. We read in ancient history that a very able king was elected by the neighing of his horse; but we shall scarcely, I think, adopt this mode of election. In one of the most celebrated republics of antiquity, Athens, Senators and Magistrates were chosen by lot; and sometimes the lot fell fortunately. Once, for example, Socrates was in office. A cruel and unjust proposition was made by a demagogue. Socrates resisted it at the hazard of his own life. There is no event in Grecian history more interesting than that memorable resistance. Yet who would have officers appointed by lot because the accident of the lot may have given to a great and good man a power which he would probably never have attained in any other way? We must judge, as I said, by the general tendency of a system. No person can doubt that a House of Commons chosen freely by the middle classes will contain many very able men. I do not say that precisely the same able men who would find their way into the present House of Commons will find their way into the reformed House; but that is not the question. No particular man is necessary to the State. We may depend on it that, if we provide the country with popular institutions, those institutions will provide it with great men.

There is another objection, which, I think, was first raised by the hon. and learned member for Newport [Mr. Horace Twiss]. He tells us that the elective franchise is property; that to take it away from a man who has not been judicially convicted of malpractices is robbery; that no crime is proved against the voters in the close boroughs; that no crime is even imputed to them in the preamble of this bill; and that therefore to disfranchise them without compensation would be an act of revolutionary tyranny. The hon. and learned gentleman has compared the conduct of the present Ministers to that of those odious tools of power who, towards the close of the reign of Charles the Second, seized the charters of the Whig Corporations. Now, there was another precedent, which I wonder that he did not recollect, both because it is much more nearly in point than that to which he referred, and because my noble friend, the Paymaster of the Forces, had previously alluded to it. If the elective franchise is property, if to disfranchise voters without a crime proved, or a compensation given, be robbery, was there ever such an act of robbery as the disfranchising of the Irish forty-shilling freeholders? Was any pecuniary compensation given to them? Is it declared in the preamble of the bill which took away their franchise that they had been convicted of any offence? Was any judicial inquiry instituted into their conduct? Were they even accused of any crime? Or if you say that it was a crime in the electors of Clare to vote for the hon. and learned gentleman who now represents the county of Waterford, was a Protestant freeholder in Louth to be punished for the crime of a Catholic freeholder in Clare? If the principle of the hon. and learned member for Newport be sound, the franchise of the Irish peasant was property. That franchise the Ministers under whom the hon. and learned member held office did not scruple to take away. Will he accuse those Ministers of robbery? If not, how can he bring such an accusation against their successors?

Every gentleman, I think, who has spoken from the other side of the House has alluded to the opinions which some of his Majesty's Ministers formerly entertained on the subject of Reform. It would be officious in me, Sir, to undertake the defence of gentlemen who are so well able to defend themselves. I will only say that, in my opinion, the country will not think worse either of their capacity or of their patriotism because they have shown that they can profit by experience, because they have learned to see the folly of delaying inevitable changes. There are others who ought to have learned the same lesson. I say, Sir, that there are those who, I should have thought, must have had enough to last them all their lives of that humiliation which follows obstinate and boastful resistance to changes rendered necessary by the progress of society, and by the development of the human mind. Is it possible that those persons can wish again to occupy a position which can neither be defended nor surrendered with honour? I well remember, Sir, a certain evening in the month of May 1827. I had not then the honour of a seat in this House, but I was an attentive observer of its proceedings. The right hon. Baronet opposite [Sir Robert Peel], of whom personally I desire to speak with that high respect which I feel for his talents and his character, but of whose public conduct I must speak with the sincerity required by my public duty, was then, as he is now, out of office. He had just resigned the seals of the Home Department, because he conceived that the recent ministerial arrangements had been too favourable to the Catholic claims. He rose to ask whether it was the intention of the new Cabinet to repeal the Test and Corporation Acts, and to reform the Parliament. He bound up, I well remember, those two questions together; and he declared that if the Ministers should either attempt to repeal the Test and Corporation Acts, or bring forward a measure of Parliamentary Reform, he should think it his duty to oppose them to the utmost. Since that declaration was made four years have elapsed; and what is now the state of the three questions which then chiefly agitated the minds of men? What is become of the Test and Corporation Acts? They are repealed. By whom? By the right hon. Baronet. What has become of the Catholic disabilities? They are removed. By whom? By the right hon. Baronet. The question of Parliamentary Reform is still behind. But signs, of which it is impossible to misconceive the import, do most clearly indicate that unless that question also be speedily settled, property and order, and all the institutions of this great monarchy, will be exposed to fearful peril. Is it possible that gentlemen long versed in high political affairs cannot read these signs? Is it possible that they can really believe that the Representative system of England, such as it now is, will last to the year 1860? If not, for what would they have us wait? Would they have us wait merely that we may show to all the world how little we have profited by our own recent experience? Would they have us wait that we may once again hit the exact point where we can neither refuse with authority nor concede with grace? Would they have us wait that the numbers of the discontented party may become larger, its demand higher, its feelings more acrimonious, its organisation more complete? Would they have us wait till the whole tragi-comedy of 1827 has been acted over again? till they have been brought into office by a cry of "No Reform," to be reformers, as they were once before brought into office by a cry of "No Popery," to be emancipators? Have they obliterated from their minds—gladly, perhaps, would some among them obliterate from their minds—the transactions of that year? And have they forgotten all the transactions of the succeeding year? Have they forgotten how the spirit of liberty in Ireland, debarred from its natural outlet, found a vent by forbidden passages? Have they forgotten how we were forced to indulge the Catholics in all the licence of rebels, merely because we chose to withhold from them the liberties of subjects? Do they wait for associations more formidable than that of the Corn Exchange, for contributions larger than the Rent, for agitators more violent than those who, three years ago, divided with the King and the Parliament the sovereignty of Ireland? Do they wait for that last and most dreadful paroxysm of popular rage, for that last and most cruel test of military fidelity? Let them wait, if their past experience shall induce them to think that any high honour or any exquisite pleasure is to be obtained by a policy like this. Let them wait, if this strange and fearful infatuation be indeed upon them, that they should not see with their eyes, or hear with their ears, or understand with their heart. But let us know our interest and our duty better. Turn where we may, within, around, the voice of great events is proclaiming to us, Reform, that you may preserve. Now, therefore, while everything at home and abroad forebodes ruin to those who persist in a hopeless struggle against the spirit of the age; now, while the crash of the proudest throne of the Continent is still resounding in our ears; now, while the roof of a British palace affords an ignominious shelter to the exiled heir of forty kings; now, while we see on every side ancient institutions subverted and great societies dissolved; now, while the heart of England is still sound; now, while old feelings and old associations retain a power and a charm which may too soon pass away; now, in this your accepted time; now, in this your day of salvation, take counsel, not of prejudice, not of party spirit, not of the ignominious pride of a fatal consistency, but of history, of reason, of the ages which are past, of the signs of this most portentous time. Pronounce in a manner worthy of the expectation with which this great debate has been anticipated, and of the long remembrance which it will leave behind. Renew the youth of the State. Save property, divided against itself. Save the multitude, endangered by its own ungovernable passions. Save the aristocracy, endangered by its own unpopular power. Save the greatest, and fairest, and most highly civilised community that ever existed from calamities which may in a few days sweep away all the rich heritage of so many ages of wisdom and glory. The danger is terrible. The time is short. If this bill should be rejected, I pray to God that none of those who concur in rejecting it may ever remember their votes with unavailing remorse amidst the wreck of laws, the confusion of ranks, the spoliation of property, and the dissolution of social order.

Five

THE CHARTIST MOVEMENT

Thomas Attwood

Thomas Attwood (1783-1856), political reformer, was a Birmingham banker who was elected to Parliament in 1832 following the passage of the Reform Bill. As an M.P. he was a radical and was associated with Daniel O'Connell in his attempt to have the Anglo-Irish union repealed. He allied himself with the Chartists and presented their petition to Parliament. Few of the M.P.'s of that day would have been willing to associate themselves with what was basically a working class movement. The monster petition was brought to the Commons in a cab and formally placed before the House. Parliament rejected the demands of the petitioners. The organizers of the movement tried again and again but were unsuccessful. However, over the next seventy-five years all of the Chartist demands were met but one; that for annual elections for Parliament. "The National Petition," *Hansard, 3rd Series,* Volume XLVIII, 1839, and *Hansard, 3rd Series,* Volume LXII, 1842.

Attwood's Speech Introducing the Charter *(14 June 1839)*

Mr. T. Attwood said, in rising to present this very extraordinary and important petition, he was aware that the rules of the House would not allow him to enter upon any general statement on the subject to which it referred, nor to go into a defence of the great principles which were there set forth. He should, there-fore, endeavour to keep strictly within the rules prescribed by the House, as the proper line of conduct to be observed by Members on presenting petitions, and confine himself to a statement of the sub-stance and contents; and then, perhaps, the House would indulge him by permitting him to say a few words—a few words only—in explanation of the circumstances as regarded his own personal position in connection with the petition. The petition originated in the town of Birmingham. It was adopted there at a very numerous meeting on the 6th of August, last year. Having been so adopted, it was then forwarded to Glasgow, where in a short time, it re-ceived no less a number than the signature of 90,000 honest, indus-trious men; and it afterwards received the signatures of nearly the same number at Birmingham and the neighbourhood of that town. He held in his hand a list of two hundred and fourteen towns and villages, in different parts of Great Britain, where the petition had been deliberately adopted and signed; and it was now presented to that House with 1,280,000 signatures, the result of not less than 500 public meetings, which had been held in support of the prin-ciples contained in this petition. At each of those meetings there had been one universal anxious cry of distress—distress he must say, long disregarded by that House, yet existing for years—distress which had caused much discontent amongst the working people, and which discontent was created by the long sufferings and griev-ances which that class of the people had endured, and so long utterly disregarded by the people's representatives in that House. (Order, order.) He hoped the House would listen to what he said, and would afford due attention to a petition so universally signed; that the House would not say, because the petitioners were merely humble working men that their opinions should be disregarded, and that their grievances should not be considered and redressed. He sincerely trusted that such would not be the case. It would be a most serious grievance and offense to these people who signed the petition, if such were to be the result in the presence of their dele-gates, who had been allowed to be present to witness its presenta-tion; and it would be most painful for him to have to state such a result, and to carry back a report to those who had intrusted the petition to his hands that it had been treated with any symptoms of disregard or disrespect by that House. The men who signed the petition were honest and industrious—of sober and unblemished character—men who have uniformly discharged the duties of good members of society and loyal subjects, and who had always obeyed the laws. Gentlemen enjoying the wealth handed down to them by hereditary descent, whose wants were provided for by the estates to which they succeeded from their forefathers, could have no idea of the privations suffered by the working men of this country. Yet at all the meetings which have been held, the persons attending them had confined themselves strictly to the legal pursuit of their constitutional rights, for the purpose of remedying the extreme sufferings which they had endured for so many years. They had seen no attempt to relieve their sufferings, whether they were hand-loom weavers, artisans, or agricultural labourers—no matter what they might be, still there was no relief. They met with no support, or even sympathy, from that House, and, therefore, they felt themselves bound to exercise every legal and constitutional effort within their power to recover the whole of their constitutional rights. All that these honest men said was, that the Members of that House by birth, parentage, habits of life, wealth, and education, had not shown that anxiety to relieve the sufferings and redress the wrongs of the working classes, which they believed to be their rights, as enjoying the privileges of British subjects. Therefore, they had adopted the extreme course of entering upon that separate path, with the view of endeavouring to recover those ancient privileges which they believed to form the original and constitutional right of the Commons of England. For many years they had hoped and trusted that such an effort on their part would not be needed. They hoped it might be spared, and they placed their confidence in that hope to the protection which they looked for, and which they were taught to expect they should receive at the hands of the gentlemen of England. He should now read a brief extract from the petition. It stated, that they only sought a fair day's wages for a fair day's work; and that if they could not give them that, and food and clothing for their families, then they said they would put forward every means which the law allowed, to change the representation of that House; that they would use every effort to act upon the electors, and that by these means ultimately, reason thus working upon influence, they should produce such a change as would enable them to succeed in the accomplishment of their views and wishes. He trusted in God they would succeed, and obtain all the objects sought for in the petition. The first thing sought for by these honest men, every one of whom produced by his labour four times more to the country than they asked for in exchange, was a fair subsistence—and yet their country refused them one-fourth of the value of their labours. Not only did the country do that, but some of them had only three days' wages in the week, and hundreds of them were paying 400 per cent. increase on debts and taxes. Such being the case, the House would not be surprised, that these honest men should have used rather strong language under trying circumstances. The first clause of the petition was for universal suffrage; that representations should be co-equal with taxation—the ancient constitutional law of England. It said, that they had been bowed down to the earth for a series of years. That capital of the master must not be deprived of due reward—that the labourer must have a return in wages for his labour—and that the laws which made money dear, and labour cheap, must be abolished. The petition next demanded universal suffrage, in the language of their forefathers, as expressed in the celebrated Petition of Right. Then it showed that the constitution guaranteed freedom of election, and contended, that to secure freedom of election, vote by ballot was absolutely necessary, and therefore vote by ballot was a constitutional right. It further declared, that agreeably to the acts of settlement, Parliaments were ordered to be triennial, or more frequent; and therefore the petition asked for annual Parliaments. Then it declared, that Members should be paid for their attendance in Parliament, as was the case in the days of Andrew Marvel, and as he might now easily establish, if he thought proper, in Birmingham. That was the ancient law. Members were paid by those who sent them to Parliament, and the petitioners were of opinion, until that right was restored, they should not have members who would properly feel and understand the wants, and real interests of the people. The fifth demand was, that the property qualification of Members should be abolished. In all these five points he most cordially agreed, and he most sincerely hoped that, by the progress of public opinion, the day might not be distant when the whole of those five points would be granted to the people; and that they would have them in full weight and measure, and no mistake about the matter.

SIR G. H. SMYTH rose to order. The hon. Member had transgressed the rules of the House. It was a distinct rule of the House, that no Member should make a speech on presenting a petition, and he could not believe that any member, with that ridiculous piece of machinery (the immense petition had been rolled into the House), would be permitted to adopt a course that had been uniformly refused to himself and others.

THE SPEAKER, as the hon. Member had appealed to him, must certainly say, that no Member had a right to speak at any length on presenting a petition. But when the House considered the circumstances of the case, and the position in which the hon. Member was placed, perhaps they would see that there were grounds for granting some indulgence in the matter.

SIR G. H. SMYTH, as an individual, must enter his protest against the course adopted by the hon. Member for Birmingham.

MR. ATTWOOD was thankful for the indulgence extended to him, and would only trespass a few minutes longer upon the attention of the House. But he wished to say a few words in explanation of his own peculiar situation. Although he most cordially supported the petition, was ready to support every word contained in it, and was determined to use every means in his power in order to carry it out into a law, he must say, that many reports had gone abroad, in regard to arguments said to have been used in support of the petition on different occasions, which he distinctly disavowed. He never, in the whole course of his life, recommended any means, or inculcated any doctrine except peace, law, order, loyalty, and union, and always in the same manner, and in the same feeling, fairly and openly doing all that he could as a man, a patriot, and a Christian, to work out the principles which he maintained, and to support the views of the petitioners. He washed his hands of any idea, of any appeal to physical force. He deprecated all such notions—he repudiated all talk of arms—he wished for no arms but the will of the people, legally, fairly, and constitutionally expressed—and if the people would only adopt his views, and respond to his voice—if they would send up similar petitions from every parish in England, and go on using ever argument which justice, reason, and wisdom dictate, they would create such an action in the public mind, which would again act upon Members of that House —that giving due allowance for the prevalence of generous feeling among English gentlemen and the English people, if the people would act in that manner—if they proceeded wisely and discreetly, washing their hands of all insolence and violence—he was confident they would ultimately secure the attentive consideration of that House. Having said so much, he should now read the prayer of the petition, which was to the following effect:—

> That it might please their honourable House to take the petition into their most serious consideration, and to use their utmost endeavour to pass a law, granting to every man of lawful age, sound mind, and uncontaminated by crime, the right of voting for Members to serve in Parliament; that they would cause a law also to be passed giving the right to vote by the ballot; that the duration of Parliaments might in no case be of greater duration than one year; that they would abolish all property qualifications, to entitle persons to sit in their honourable House; and that all Members elected to sit in Parliament, should be paid for their services.

He would trespass no longer on their time, but move, that the petition be now brought up. This produced loud laughter, from the gigantic dimensions of the petition. The hon. Member unrolled a sufficient portion of it to enable him to place one extremity of it on the clerk's table.

Petition to be printed.

To the Honourable the Commons of Great Britain and Ireland, Parliament Assembled.

The Petition of the undersigned people of the United Kingdom,

Sheweth—That Government originated from, was designed to protect the freedom and promote the happiness of, and ought to be responsible to, the whole people.

That the only authority on which any body of men can make laws and govern society, is delegation from the people.

That as Government was designed for the benefit and protection of, and must be obeyed and supported by all, therefore all should be equally represented.

That any form of Government which fails to effect the purposes for which it was designed, and does not fully and completely represent the whole people, who are compelled to pay taxes to its support and obey the laws resolved upon by it, is unconstitutional, tyrannical, and ought to be amended or resisted.

That your honourable House, as at present constituted, has not been elected by, and acts irresponsibly of, the people; and hitherto has only represented parties, and benefitted the few, regardless of the miseries, grievances, and petitions of the many. Your honourable House has enacted laws contrary to the expressed wishes of the people, and by unconstitutional means enforced obedience to them, thereby creating an unbearable despotism on the one, and degrading slavery on the other.

That if your honourable House is of opinion that the people of Great Britain and Ireland ought not to be fully represented, your petitioners pray that such opinion may be unequivocally made known, that the people may fully understand what they can or cannot expect from your honourable House: because if such be the decision of your honourable House, your petitioners are of opinion that where representation is denied, taxation ought to be resisted.

That your petitioners instance, in proof of their assertion, that your honourable House has not been elected by the people; that the population of Great Britain and Ireland is at the present time about twenty-six millions of persons; and that yet, out of this number, little more than nine hundred thousand have been permitted to vote in the recent election of representatives to make laws to govern the whole.

That the existing state of representation is not only extremely limited and unjust, but unequally divided, and gives preponderating influence to the landed and monied interests to the utter ruin of the small-trading and labouring classes.

That the borough of Guildford, with a population of 3,920 returns to Parliament as many members as the Tower Hamlets, with a population of 300,000; Evesham, with a population of 3,998 elects as many representatives as Manchester, with a population of 200,000; and Buckingham, Evesham, Totness, Guildford, Honiton, and Bridport, with a total population of 23,000, return as many representatives as Manchester, Finsbury, Tower Hamlets, Liverpool, Marylebone, and Lambeth, with a population of 1,400,000: these being but a very few instances of the enormous inequalities existing in what is called the representation of this country.

That bribery, intimidation, corruption, perjury, and riot prevail at all parliamentary elections, to an extent best understood by the Members of your honourable House.

That your petitioners complain that they are enormously taxed to pay the interest of what is termed the national debt, a debt amounting at present to £800,000,000, being only a portion of the enormous amount expended in cruel and expensive wars for the suppression of all liberty, by men not authorised by the people, and who, consequently, had no right to tax posterity for the outrages committed by them upon mankind. And your petitioners loudly complain of the augmentation of that debt, after twenty-six years of almost uninterrupted peace, and whilst poverty and discontent rage over the land.

That taxation, both general and local, is at this time too enormous to be borne; and in the opinion of your petitioners is contrary to the spirit of the Bill of Rights, wherein it is clearly expressed that no subject shall be compelled to contribute to any tax, talliage, or aid, unless imposed by common consent in Parliament.

That in England, Ireland, Scotland, and Wales, thousands of people are dying from actual want; and your petitioners, whilst sensible that poverty is the great existing cause of crime, view with mingled astonishment and alarm the ill provision made for the poor, the aged, the infirm; and likewise perceive, with feelings of indignation, the determination of the honourable House to continue the Poor-law Bill in operation, notwithstanding the many proofs which have been afforded by sad experience of the unconstitutional principle of that bill, of its unchristian character, and of the cruel and murderous effects produced upon the wages of working men, and the lives of the subjects of this realm.

That your petitioners conceive that bill to be contrary to all previous statutes, opposed to the spirit of the constitution, and in actual violation of the precepts of the Christian religion; and, therefore, your petitioners look with apprehension to the results which may flow from its continuance.

That your petitioners would direct the attention of your honourable House to the great disparity existing between the wages of the producing millions, and the salaries of those whose comparative usefulness ought to be questioned, where riches and luxury prevail amongst the rulers, and poverty and starvation amongst the ruled.

That your petitioners, with all due respect and loyalty, would compare the daily income of the Sovereign Majesty with that of thousands of the working men of this nation; and whilst your petitioners have learned that her Majesty receives daily for her private use the sum of £164. 17s. 10d., they have also ascertained that many thousands of the families of the labourers are only in the receipt of 3¾d. per head per day.

That your petitioners have also learned that his royal Highness Prince Albert receives each day the sum of £104. 2s., whilst thousands have to exist upon 3d. per head per day.

That your petitioners have also heard with astonishment, that the King of Hanover daily receives £57. 10s., whilst thousands of the tax-payers of this empire live upon 2¾d. per head per day.

That your petitioners have with pain and regret, also learned that the Archbishop of Canterbury is daily in the receipt of £52. 10s. per day, whilst thousands of the poor have to maintain their families upon an income not exceeding 2d. per head per day.

That notwithstanding the wretched and unparalleled condition of the people, your honourable House has manifested no disposition to curtail the expenses of the State, to diminish taxation, or promote general prosperity.

That unless immediate remedial measures be adopted, your petitioners fear the increasing distress of the people will lead to results fearful to contemplate; because your petitioners can produce evidence of the gradual decline of wages, at the same time that the constant increase of the national burdens must be apparent to all.

That your petitioners know that it is the undoubted constitutional right of the people, to meet freely, when, how, and where they choose, in public places, peaceably, in the day, to discuss their grievances, and political or other subjects, or for the purpose of framing, discussing, or passing any vote, petition, or remonstrance, upon any subject whatsoever.

That your petitioners complain that the right has unconstitutionally been infringed; and 500 well disposed persons have been arrested, excessive bail demanded, tried by packed juries, sentenced to imprisonment, and treated as felons of the worst description.

That an unconstitutional police force is distributed all over the country, at enormous cost, to prevent the due exercise of the people's rights. And your petitioners are of opinion that the Poor-law Bastiles and the police stations, being co-existent, have originated from the same cause, viz., the increased desire on the part of the irresponsible few to oppress and starve the many.

That a vast and unconstitutional army is upheld at the public expense, for the purpose of repressing public opinion in the three kingdoms, and likewise to intimidate the millions in the due exercise of those rights and privileges which ought to belong to them.

That your petitioners complain that the hours of labour, particularly of the factory workers, are protracted beyond the limits of human endurance, and that the wages earned, after unnatural application to toil in heated and unhealthy workshops, are inadequate to sustain the bodily strength, and supply those comforts which are so imperative after an excessive waste of physical energy.

That your petitioners also direct the attention of your honourable House to the starvation wages of the agricultural labourer, and view with horror and indignation the paltry income of those whose toil gives being to the staple food of this people.

That your petitioners deeply deplore the existence of any kind of monopoly in this nation, and whilst they unequivocally condemn the levying of any tax upon the necessaries of life, and upon those articles principally required by the labouring classes, they are also sensible that the abolition of any one monopoly will never unshackle labour from its misery until the people possess that power under which all monopoly and oppression must cease; and your petitioners respectfully mention the existing monopolies of the suffrage, of paper money, of machinery, of land, of the public press, of religious privileges, of the means of travelling and transit, and of a host of other evils too numerous to mention, all arising from class legislation, but which your honourable House has always consistently endeavoured to increase instead of diminish.

That your petitioners are sensible, from the numerous petitions presented to your honourable House, that your honourable House is fully acquainted with the grievances of the working men; and your petitioners pray that the rights and wrongs of labour may be considered, with a view to protection of the one, and to the removal of the other; because your petitioners are of opinion that it is the worst species of legislation which leaves the grievances of society to be removed only by violence or revolution, both of which may be apprehended if complaints are unattended to and petitions despised.

That your petitioners complain that upwards of nine millions of pounds per annum are unjustly abstracted from them to maintain a church establishment, from which they principally dissent; and beg to call the attention of your honourable House to the fact, that this enormous sum is equal to, if it does not exceed, the cost of upholding Christianity in all parts of the world beside. Your petitioners complain that it is unjust, and not in accordance with the Christian religion, to enforce compulsory support of religious creeds, and expensive church establishments, with which the people do not agree.

That your petitioners believe all men have a right to worship God as may appear best to their consciences, and that no legislative enactments should interfere between man and his Creator.

That your petitioners direct the attention of your honourable House to the enormous revenue annually swallowed up by the bishops and the clergy, and entreat you to contrast their deeds with the conduct of the founder of the Christian religion, who denounced worshippers of Mammon, and taught charity, meekness, and brotherly love.

That your petitioners strongly complain that the people of this kingdom are subject to the rule of irresponsible law-makers to whom they have given no authority, and are enormously taxed to uphold a corrupt system, to which they have never in person or by representation given their assent.

That your petitioners maintain that it is the inherent, indubitable, and constitutional right, founded upon the ancient practice of the realm of England, and supported by well approved statutes, of every male inhabitant of the United Kingdom, he being of age and of sound mind, non-convict of crime, and not confined under any judicial process, to exercise the elective franchise in the choice of Members to serve in the Commons House of Parliament.

That your petitioners can prove, that by the ancient customs and statutes of this realm, Parliament should be held once in each year.

That your petitioners maintain that Members elected to serve in Parliament ought to be the servants of the people, and should, at short and stated intervals, return to their constituencies, to ascertain if their conduct is approved of, and to give the people power to reject all who have not acted honestly and justly.

That your petitioners complain that possession of property is made the test of men's qualification to sit in Parliament.

That your petitioners can give proof that such qualification is irrational, unnecessary, and not in accordance with the ancient usages of England.

That your petitioners complain, that by influence, patronage, and intimidation, there is at present no purity of election; and your petitioners contend for the right of voting by ballot.

That your petitioners complain that seats in your honourable House are sought for at a most extravagant rate of expense; which proves an enormous degree of fraud and corruption.

That your petitioners, therefore, contend, that to put an end to secret political traffic, all representatives should be paid a limited amount for their services.

That your petitioners complain of the many grievances borne by the people of Ireland, and contend that they are fully entitled to a repeal of the legislative union.

That your petitioners have viewed with great indignation that partiality shown to the aristocracy in the courts of justice, and the cruelty of that system of law which deprived Frost, Williams, and Jones, of the benefit of their objection offered by Sir Frederick Pollock during the trial at Monmouth, and which was approved of by the large majority of the judges.

That your petitioners beg to assure your honourable House that they cannot, within the limits of this their petition, set forth even a tithe of the many grievances of which they may justly complain; but should your honourable House be pleased to grant your petitioners a hearing by representatives at the Bar of your honourable House, your petitioners will be enabled to unfold a tale of wrong and suffering—of intolerable injustice—which will create utter astonishment in the minds of all benevolent and good men, that the people of Great Britain and Ireland have so long quietly endured their wretched condition, brought upon them as it has been by unjust exclusion from political authority, and by the manifold corruptions of class-legislation.

That your petitioners, therefore, exercising their just constitutional right, demand that your honourable House do remedy the many gross and manifest evils of which your petitioners complain, do immediately, without alteration, deduction, or addition, pass into a law the document entitled 'The People's Charter,' which embraces the representation of male adults, vote by ballot, annual Parliaments, no property qualification, payment of Members, and equal electoral districts.

And that your petitioners, desiring to promote the peace of the United Kingdom, security of property, and prosperity of commerce, seriously and earnestly press this, their petition, on the attention of your honourable House.

Six

EMPLOYMENT
OF CHILDREN

Lord Ashley

Antony Ashley Cooper, seventh Earl of Shaftesbury (1801-1885), philanthropist, was educated at Oxford University. He was elected to Parliament in 1826 and retained his seat until 1851 when he succeeded his father to the peerage. He was an active reformer throughout his entire life, urging protection of colliery workers, factory workers, and chimney sweeps, advocating creation of the so-called ragged-schools to educate the poor, and promoting public housing and improved sanitation. He was actively associated with Edwin Chadwick and the public health movement. In 1856 he was appointed chairman of the sanitary commission in the Crimea where he loyally supported the reforms proposed by Florence Nightingale. His motion for a further commission to study the workings of the Factory Act of 1833 showed Shaftesbury at his best; he did not just take up a liberal cause, have some success with it and then let it die, but instead retained his interest and worked to ensure the continued success of his efforts. Shaftesbury was a curious person in many ways. He was a complete aristocrat; he disliked unions; although he finally joined the Whig party, he was more of a Tory than Peel; he had the same high sense of duty as Wellington; and he was somewhat narrow in religion. He succeeded where others failed largely because everyone recognized that he was without personal interest and that he hated cruelty. Further, he had impeccable political connections, being the son-in-law of Lord Palmerston and at the same time a friend of Wellington. He was also much supported by the Crown and by the Prince Consort in particular. His Commission of Inquiry, introduced on August 4, 1840, was ultimately to lead to further legislation protecting the worker, such as the Mines Act of 1842, the reduction of hours for women and children in 1844, the Ten Hours Act of 1847, and the Coal Mines Inspection Act of 1850. "Employment of Children," 4 August, 1840, *Hansard, 3rd Series,* Volume LV, 1840.

Lord *Ashley* spoke as follows: It is, Sir, with feelings somewhat akin to despair, that I now rise to bring before the House, the motion of which I have given notice. When I consider the period of the Session, the long discussions that have already taken place to-day, the scanty attendance of Members, and the power which any Member possesses of stopping me midway in my career, I cannot but entertain misgivings, that I shall not be able to bring, under the attention of the House, this subject, which has now occupied so large a portion of my public life, and in which are now concentrated, in one hour, the labours of years. Sir, I must assure the House, that this motion has not been conceived, nor will it be introduced, in any hostile spirit towards Her Majesty's Ministers; quite the reverse. I do indeed trust, nay more, I have reason to believe, that I shall obtain their hearty and effectual support. Sir, I know well that I owe an apology and an explanation to the House for trespassing on their patience at so late a period—my explanation is this: I have long been taunted with narrow and exclusive attentions to the children in the factories alone; I have been told, in language and writing, that there are other cases fully as grievous, and not less numerous; that I was unjust and inconsiderate in my denouncement of the one, and my omission of the other. I have, however, long contemplated this effort which I am now making; I had long resolved that, so soon as I could see the factory children, as it were, safe in harbour, I would undertake a new task. The committee of this Session on mills and factories, having fully substantiated the necessity, and rendered certain the amendment of the law, I am now endeavouring to obtain an inquiry into the actual circumstances and condition of another large part of our juvenile population. Sir, I hardly know

whether any argument is necessary to prove that the future hopes
of a country must, under God, be laid in the character and condition of its children; however right it may be to attempt, it is
almost fruitless to expect, the reformation of its adults; as the
sapling has been bent, so will it grow. To ensure a vigorous and
moral manhood, we must train them aright from their earliest
years, and so reserve the full development of their moral and
physical energies for the service hereafter of our common country.
Now, Sir, whatever may be done or proposed in time to come, we
have, I think, a right to know the state of our juvenile population;
the House has a right, the country has a right. How is it possible to
address ourselves to the remedies of evils which we all feel, unless
we have previously ascertained both the nature and the cause of
them? The first step towards a cure is a knowledge of the disorder.
We have asserted these truths in our factory legislation; and I
have on my side, the authority of all civilized nations of modern
times; the practice of this House; the common sense of the thing;
and the justice of the principle. Sir, I may say with Tacitus, *"opus
adgredior, opimum casibus . . . ipsa etiam pace sævum:"* to give
but an outline of all the undertaking, would occupy too much of
your time and patience; few persons, perhaps, have an idea of the
number and variety of the employments which demand and ex-
haust the physical energies of young children, or of the extent of
suffering to which they are exposed. It is right, Sir, that the country
should know at what cost its pre-eminence is purchased,

> Petty rogues submit to fate,
> That great ones may enjoy their state.

The number I cannot give with any degree of accuracy, though
I may venture to place them as many-fold the numbers of those
engaged in the factories—the suffering I can exhibit, to a certain
degree, in the documents before me. Sir, I will just read a list of
some of these occupations, as many as I have been able to collect;
but I will abstain from entering into detail upon every one of
them: I will select a few instances, and leave the House to judge
of the mass by the form and taste of the sample. Now, this is a

list of some of the occupations in which I find them engaged (I have not, by any means, a full statement); and in which the employment is both irksome and unhealthy:—

> Earthenware, porcelain, hosiery, pin-making, needle-making, manufacture of arms, nail-making, card-setting, draw-boy-weaving, iron-works, forges, &c., iron foundries, glass trade, collieries, calico-printing, tobacco manufacture, button factories, bleaching, and paper-mills.

Now, Sir, will the House allow me to set before them, in a few cases, the evidence I have been able to obtain illustrative of the nature and effects of these several departments of industry? The first I shall take is the manufacture of tobacco, a business of which, perhaps, but little is generally known; in this I find that—

> Children are employed twelve hours a-day. They go as early as seven years of age. The smell in the room is very strong and offensive. They are employed in spinning the twist tobacco; in the country, the children work more hours in the day, being frequently until nine and ten o'clock at night. Their opportunities for education are almost none, and their appearance altogether sickly.

The next department I shall take is that of bleaching. In bleaching—

> Children are employed at eleven, and oftentimes younger. They go to work at any time of the day or night, when they have a deal of work. The same children labour all night for two or three nights in a week. Their opportunities for education very few, except in a Sunday school.

Now, here let the House observe the extent of toil and of watchfulness oftentimes imposed on children of very tender years. During two or three nights in a week, they are deprived altogether of their natural rest; a demand so severe on the bodily powers, that, when exacted of the police and soldiery of this metropolis, it has been found most pernicious to their physical constitution. From the Potteries, Mr. Spencer (a factory commissioner) reported, in 1833:—

The plate-makers of most works employ boys, often their own, to be their assistants; their occupation is to remove the plates to the drying houses, which are heated to 120 degrees; and in this occupation, in which the boy is kept on the run, he is laboriously employed from six o'clock in the morning till seven in the evening, excepting the intervals of breakfast and dinner. (Again), In other works some of the children called cutters, in attendance upon the printer, appear to me to suffer from a prolonged attendance at the factory. They are compelled to attend in the morning an hour before the printer, to light fires and prepare his apartment, and often wait in the evening for some time after the rest have departed, to prepare for the ensuing day. (Again), When there is a fair demand, the plate-makers and their assistants, work three or four nights per week till ten, and sometimes as late as eleven.

Sir, I will proceed. On the subject of Draw-boy-weaving, Mr. Horner and Mr. Woolriche reported from Kidderminster in 1833:—

Every weaver of Brussels carpeting must have an assistant, called a drawer, who is usually a boy or girl; few are taken under ten years of age; the working hours are extremely irregular; this irregularity tells very severely on the drawers, who must attend the weaver at whatever time he is at work; they are often called up at three and four o'clock in the morning, and kept on for sixteen or eighteen hours.

With respect to the iron foundries I have not obtained any evidence; though much, I am sure, would be derived from an investigation of this department. As to iron mines, it will be unnecessary to do much more than simply refer the House to a report from the mining districts of South Wales, by Mr. Seymour Tremenheere, the Government-inspector, dated February, 1840, and published in the extracts from the proceedings of the Board of Privy Council on the matter of education. I will, however, take the liberty to read one or two extracts:—

Parents, (says the Inspector), if they send their children at all to school, seldom do so for many months at a time. They are liable to be away whenever the father has not earned as much as usual, or has spent more. They think instruction of any kind very little necessary for the girls. The boys are taken into the coal or iron mine at eight or nine years old.

Elsewhere he says:—

Hence the custom of taking their children of seven years old, to sit for eight and ten hours a day in the mine; it is certain from the time he (the child) enters the mine, he learns nothing more there than to be a miner.

Now let the House hear the consequences of this defect of education—the result of this overwork in the first years of life:—

They leave their homes at an early age, and they spend the surplus of their wages in smoking, drinking, and quarrelling. Boys of thirteen will not unfrequently boast that they have taken to smoking before they were twelve. Early marriages are very frequent. They take their wives from the coke hearths, the mine, and coal-yard, having had no opportunities of acquiring any better principles or improved habits of domestic economy, and being in all other respects less instructed than their husbands.

As to the frame-work-knitters, a department of the lace trade, nothing can be worse or more distressing. Mr. Power, a factory commissioner, wrote from Nottingham, 1833:—

A great proportion of the population of the county of Leicester is employed in the frame-work, knitting; of this number more than one-half, probably two-thirds, are young persons between the ages of six and eighteen; that they work an inordinate number of hours daily; that the hours of work of the young persons are, for the most part, commensurate with those of the older class; that the occupation is pursued in very low and confined shops and rooms, and that the hours of labour are sixteen in the day. With regard to the state of health of men, women, and children employed, their habits of work and subsistence are more destructive of health, comfort, cleanliness, and general well being, than any state of employment into which I have had at present an opportunity of inquiring. Mr. Macaulay, a surgeon of great talent and experience at Leicester, observed to me, that scarcely any of them of long-standing in the trade were quite sound in constitution.

Sir, there is another department of industry called card-setting, in which children are employed to make part of the machinery of the cotton-mills. In answer to some questions I put to a gentleman resident in the neighbourhood of some card-setting establishments, he says:—

> Children are employed from five years old and upwards; their length of labour extends from five or six o'clock in the morning to eight at night.

I will now, Sir, exhibit the state of the collieries, and I cannot well imagine any thing worse than these painful disclosures. In reference to this, I will read an abstract of evidence collected from three witnesses by Mr. Tuffnell, in 1833:—

> Labour very hard, nine hours a day regularly, sometimes twelve, sometimes above thirteen hours; stop two or three minutes to eat; some days nothing at all to eat, sometimes work and eat together; have worked a whole day together without stopping to eat; a good many children in the mines, some under six years of age; sometimes can't eat, owing to the dust, and damp, and badness of the air; sometimes it is as hot as an oven, sometimes so hot as to melt a candle. A vast many girls in the pits go down just the same as the boys, by ladders or baskets; the girls wear breeches; beaten the same as the boys; many bastards produced in the pits; a good deal of fighting amongst them; much crookedness caused by the labour; work by candlelight; exposed to terrible accidents; work in very contracted spaces; children are plagued with sore feet and gatherings. "I cannot but think, (says one witness), that many nights they do not sleep with a whole skin, for their backs get cut and bruised with knocking against the mine, it is so low. It is wet under foot; the water oftentimes runs down from the roof; many lives lost in various ways; and many severely injured by burning; workers knocked up after fifty." I cannot much err, (says Mr. Commissioner Tuffnell), in coming to the conclusion, both from what I say, and the evidence of witnesses given on oath above, that it must appear to every impartial judge of the two occupations, that the hardest labour, in the worst room, in the worst conducted factory, is less hard, less cruel, and less demoralizing, then the labour of the best of coal mines.

Now, Sir, the next is a trade to which I must request the particular attention of the House. The scenes it discloses are really horrible; and all who hear me will join in one loud and common condemnation. I speak of the business of pinmaking. Several witnesses in 1833 stated that:—

> It is very unwholesome work; we do it near the wire-works, and the smell of the aquafortis, through which the wire passes is a very great nuisance. Children go at a very early age, at five years old, and work from six in the morning till eight at night. There are as many girls as boys.

One witness, a pin-header, aged twelve, said:—

> I have seen the children much beaten ten times a-day, so that with some the blood comes, many a time; none of the children where I work can read or write.

Another witness said:—

> It is a sedentary employment, requiring great stress upon the eyes, and a constant motion of the foot, finger, and eyes.

This is fully confirmed in a letter I have just received; there it is stated:—

> Eye-sight is much affected, the overseers of the poor have sent many cases of this nature to the eye institution of Manchester. Each child (reports Mr. Commissioner Tuffnell), is in a position continually bent in the form of the letter C, its head being about eight inches from the table. My inquiries (he adds), fully corroborated the account of its being the practice of parents to borrow sums of money on the credit of their children's labour, and then let them out to pin heading till it is paid. One woman had let out both her children for ten months, and another had sold hers for a year.

Now I must entreat the attention of hon. Members to this system of legalized slavery; and I cannot better invite it, than by reading an extract from a letter which I have lately received:—

> You also know (says my informant), the practice of the masters in securing the services of these little slaves. One man in this town em-

ploys from four to five hundred of them. A very ordinary practice is, for the master to send for the parents or guardians, offer them an advance of money, an irresistible temptation, and then extract a bond, which the magistrates enforce, that the repayment of the loan shall be effected through the labour of the child. A child of tender age can rarely earn more than from 9d. to 1s. a-week. Thus the master becomes bodily possessor of the children as his *bona fide* slaves, and works them according to his pleasure.

And now mark this:—

If he continues, with the employment to pay wages, and keep the loan hanging over the head of the parents, who do not refuse to take the wages, yet cannot repay the loan, the masters may keep possession of the child as his slave, for an indefinite time. This is done to a great extent; the relieving-officer has tried in vain to break through the iniquitous practice; but it seems that the magistrates have not power to do it.

Now, Sir, may I ask, is this not a system of legalized slavery? Is not this a state of things which demands the interposition of Parliament, or at least an investigation, that we may know to what an extent these horrid practices have been carried? Surely the House will not now be astonished at the concluding remark of Mr. Tuffnell's report:—

Knowing (says he), the cruelties that are sometime practised, in order to keep those infants at work, I was not surprised at being told by a manufacturer, that he had left the trade, owing to the disgust he felt at this part of the business.

Let me conclude this branch of the subject by an extract from a letter descriptive of these works:—

These children are collected in rooms varying in size, height, and ventilation; the filthy state and foul atmosphere of some of these places is very injurious to the health of the children—they are filled to a most unwholesome extent. No education during the week, and very few go to a Sunday-school. I can only tell you, that from my own observation of the effect of the trade as now carried on, I do not hesitate to say, that it is the cause of utter ruin, temporal and spiritual, to eight out of every ten children that are employed in it.

This, Sir, is the language of a gentleman of great experience, and very conversant too with the temporal and spiritual condition of the poorer classes of whom he is speaking. Sir, the next and last trade which I shall now describe, is the calico printing; a business which demands the labour of several thousand children. Mr. Horner, in an admirable pamphlet, which he has recently published, on the subject of infant labour, both at home and abroad, says:—

> It is by no means uncommon for children to work as teer-boys as early as six and seven years of age, and sometimes as young as five. Children of six, seven, and eight years old, may be seen going to work at—

What hour will the House think? at what hour of a winter's night? or at what hour of the night at all? Why, he proceeds:—

> At twelve o'clock of a winter's night, in large numbers, sometimes having to walk a mile or two to the works. When they are twelving, the first set goes at twelve o'clock in the day, and works till twelve at night. Sometimes they do not send away those who have worked from twelve in the day to twelve at night, but let them sleep a few hours in the works, and then set them on again. There is no interval for meals in the night set, except breakfast, the children taking something with them; and even their breakfast is taken at the works. The custom of taking their meals in the works is very injurious, for they do not wash their hands, and they consequently sometimes swallow deleterious colouring matter.

A person whose name is not given, states, that:—

> Being frequently detained in his counting-house late at night, till twelve or one o'clock, he has often, in going home in the depth of winter, met mothers taking their children to the neighbouring print-works, the children crying.

All this I can confirm and exceed, by the statements of a letter I hold in my hand, from a medical gentleman, living in the very centre of print works. I wish there were time to read the whole of it, but I fear I have already fatigued the House by the number of my extracts:—

> Many children (he writes), are only six years of age; one-half of them, he believes, are under nine; the labour of children is not only harder, but of longer duration. During night-work the men are obliged to shake their teerers to keep them awake, and they are not seldom aroused by blows. This work is very fatiguing to the eyes, their sight consequently fails at a very early age. They have to clean the blocks; this is done at the margin of the brook, on which the works stand. I often see these little creatures standing up to the calves of their legs in the water, and this, even in the severest weather, after being kept all day in rooms heated to a most oppressive degree. The injurious effect of this close and heated atmosphere is much aggravated by the effluvia of the colours; these are in most cases metallic salts, and . . . very noxious. The atmosphere of the room is consequently continually loaded with poisonous gases of different kinds.

Sir, these are a few facts, and only a few, of the many that I could adduce for your consideration, were I not afraid of being wearisome to the House. But I think I have sufficiently proved, that there prevails a system of slavery under the sanction of law; that parents sell the services of their children, even of the tenderest years, for periods of long and most afflicting duration; that, in many instances, children of not more than five or six years old are employed in these trades from twelve to sixteen hours a-day, of course deprived of all means of education, while their health is undermined, or utterly destroyed. If the inquiry I move for be granted, it will develop, I am sure, cases far more numerous, and quite as painful, as those I have been able to produce. Now, Sir, I may be called upon to suggest a remedy; Sir, I am not yet prepared to do so, but I will state my objects, and the motives of my proposition. My first and great object is to place, if possible, the children of this land in such a position, and under such circumstances, as to lay them open to what Dr. Chalmers would call "an aggressive movement" for education; to reserve and cherish their physical energies, to cultivate and improve their moral part, both of which, be they taken separately or conjointly, are essential to the peace, security, and progress of the empire. Sir, we have had the honour of setting the example in these things, and other nations of the world have begun to follow that example; we must not now fall back into the rear, and become the last where once we were first. Sir, I have here a most valuable document, for which I am indebted to the kindness of that distinguished Frenchman, the Baron Charles Dupin; it is the Report of a Commission of the Chamber of Peers, dated February, 1840, on the propriety, nay, the necessity, of extending the protection of the laws to the young and helpless workers in all departments of industry.

What is the state of morality, (says the document), among the young children employed in the workshops?—None at all; everywhere there is want. It is a curious fact, (the reporter adds), that the immorality seems to be greatest in those very places where the children are admitted into the workshops at the earliest ages.

Now let the House pay attention to what follows.

We were desirous of ascertaining the amount of difference in force and physical power between parties which had respectively attained the age of manhood in the parts of France most devoted to agriculture, and those where manufacturing industry is more generally diffused. The councils of revision in the recruiting department exhibited the following facts:—For 10,000 young men capable of military service, there were rejected as infirm or otherwise unfit in body, 4,029 in the departments most agricultural; for 10,000 in the departments most manufacturing there were rejected, 9,930.

The reporter then proceeds to speak in detail.

There were found, (he says) for 10,000 capable of military service, in Marne 10,309 incapable; in the Lower Seine 11,990 incapable; in L'Eure 14,451 incapable.

After such a statement as this, will not the House be prepared to concur in his closing observation:—

These deformities cannot allow the Legislature to remain indifferent; they attest the deep and painful mischiefs, they reveal the intolerable nature of individual suffering, they enfeeble the country in respect of its capacity for military operations, and impoverish it in regard to the works of peace. We should blush for agriculture, if in her operations she brought, at the age adapted to labour, so small a proportion of horses or oxen in a fit state for toil, compared with so large a number of infirm or misshapen.

Doubtless, Sir, if we could conduct the same investigation (which, I fear, we have not the means of doing), we should obtain, in respect of the greater extent, and longer prevalence of these trades among us, far more distressing results;—this report, I must say, is most honourable to the Chamber of Peers, most honourable to the Baron Dupin, and it will be honourable to the French nation, if they adopt the advice, and enact the provisions suggested by these wise and excellent statesmen. Sir, I next desire to remove these spectacles of suffering and oppression from the eyes of the poorer classes, or at least to ascertain if we can do so; these things perplex the peaceable, and exasperate the discontented; they have a tendency to render capital odious, for wealth is known to them only by its oppressions; they judge of it by what they see immediately around them; they know but little beyond their own narrow sphere; they do not extend their view over the whole surface of the land, and so perceive and understand the compensating advantages that wealth and poverty bestow on the community at large. Sir, with so much ignorance on one side, and so much oppression on the other, I have never wondered that perilous errors and bitter hatreds have prevailed; but I have wondered much, and been very thankful that they have prevailed so little. Again, Sir, this inquiry is due also to the other branches of trade and manufacture, which are already restricted in their employment of children by the acts of the Legislature—it is requisite we should know how far the exception operates unfavourably on the restricted trades, and how far it impedes the full development of the protective principles of existing laws. Manufacturers, I know, loudly complain, and I think with some reason. A respectable mill-owner in the West Riding of Yorkshire writes to me.

When the cotton trade is brisk, we find the demand for young persons to set cards so great, that hands are with difficulty obtained for woollen-mills in this neighbourhood.

The House will with difficulty believe, for how minute an addition to the daily wages, parents will doom their children to excessive labour.

The proprietor of a large cotton-mill told me, (says Mr. Horner,) that they suffer severely from the neighbouring printworks carrying off the children under thirteen years of age, where they employ them at any age and any number of hours; that they would gladly employ two sets of children, each working half a day, both for the sake of their work, and for the sake of the children themselves, that they might be more at school, and have more play, but that they cannot get them, as the printworks carry them off.

No doubt, Sir, provisions still more beneficial to the children, and more convenient to the mill-owners, might be introduced, under a more wide-spread system of restriction—the supply of hands for moderate toil would be increased, and more work would be done, at far less expense of health and happiness. Sir, I next propose by this inquiry, and the remedy which may follow, to enlarge the sphere of safe and useful employments. How many are there now, to which no one of principle or common humanity would consign the children! by this excessive toil, moreover, one unhappy infant does the work of two; redress this grievance, and you will have opened a comparatively safe and healthy career to twice as many children as can now be employed. I have heard, on the authority of the Poor-law Commissioners, that they have now under their guardianship more than 30,000 children, for whom they must provide a calling; they hesitate, and most laudable is their hesitation, to consign these helpless infants to such a destiny; why, will the House listen to a statement I received only a few mornings ago? It is well worthy of your attention, as showing how this system has proceeded to so frightful an extent, that even persons, whose interest it is to get rid of the children, shrink from the responsibility of exposing them to its horrors.

I have now, (says my informant), made more minute inquiry into this business of wholesale demoralization. I have examined the relieving-officer of the board of guardians. He assures me, that he has rarely known an instance of children in a family turning out respectable members of a society, who have been brought up in pin-shops; that the board of guardians have been obliged to give up the sending children from the poor-house to the pin-works, on account of the invariable consequences of it—the entire corruption of the children; and that children, once contaminated in these works, very rarely are found worth having in factories or elsewhere.

Now, Sir, if this be the case; if the children be thus contaminated by the employment of their earliest years; if they really become not worth having in factories or elsewhere, what kind of citizens will they make in after life? what has this country to hope for in their peaceful obedience or beneficial activity? Next, Sir, I hope to trace some of the secret and efficient causes of crime and pauperism; and by learning the causes, to ascertain the remedy. It is very curious and very instructive to observe how we compel, as it were, vice and misery with one hand, and endeavour to repress them with the other; but the whole course of our manufacturing system tends to these results: you engage children from their earliest and tenderest years in these long, painful, and destructive occupations; when they have approached to manhood, they have outgrown their employments, and they are turned upon the world without moral, without professional education; the business they have learned, avails them nothing; to what can they turn their hands for a maintenance? the children, for instance, who have been taught to make pins, having reached fourteen or fifteen years of age, are unfit to make pins any longer; to procure an honest livelihood then becomes to them almost impossible; the governors of prisons will tell you, the relieving-officers will tell you, that the vicious resort to plunder and prostitution; the rest sink down into a hopeless pauperism. Again, Sir, intemperance, the besetting sin of England, and the cause of many of its woes, is itself the result, in many cases, of our system of labour; just hear the effects of it in one department. The letter I shall quote, refers, it is true, to calico-printing only; it furnishes, nevertheless, a very good example of the effects of that unhealthy and prolonged toil I have endeavoured to describe.

> The most prominent evil, (says the writer,) is the excitement to habits of intoxication. The heated atmosphere in which they work, and the profuse perspiration, occasion a burning thirst; and the mouth and throat are often so parched, as to cause a very distressing sensation; they drink excessively; on leaving their highly-heated workshops, they feel disagreeably chilled, and relieve it by taking spirits. A tendency to drunkenness is thus produced; the drunkenness, gambling, and vicious habits of the men, are imitated by too many of the children.

Imitated by the children, to be sure they are—but such is our system; we not only withdraw them, when young and pliable, from the opportunities, at least, of doing good, but we thrust them, unwatched and uncared for, into dens of vice, and misery, and crime. —I should indeed be glad to read the whole of this admirable letter, but I have already trespassed too long on the indulgence of the House. These things, Mr. Speaker, at all times worthy of deep and anxious consideration, are now ten-fold so, when we remember the vast and rapid tendency there is in the present day to multiply infant labour, to the exclusion of that of adults; the House is, perhaps, but little aware of the mighty progress that has been made during the last fifteen years, towards the substitution of the sinews of the merest children for the sinews of their parents. Lastly, Sir, my object is to appeal to, and excite the public opinion; where we cannot legislate, we can exhort, and laws may fail, where example will succeed. I must appeal to the bishops and ministers of the Church of England, nay, more, to the ministers of every denomination, to urge on the hearts of their hearers, the mischief and the danger of these covetous and cruel practices; I trust they will not fall short of the zeal and eloquence of a distinguished prelate in a neighbouring country, who, in these beautiful and emphatic words, exhorted his hearers to justice and mercy:

> Open your eyes, (says the Prince Archbishop), and behold; parents and masters demand of these young plants to produce fruit in the season of blossoms. By excessive and prolonged labour they exhaust the rising sap, caring but little that they leave them to vegetate and

perish on a withered and tottering stem. Poor little children! may the laws hasten to extend their protection over your existence, and may posterity read with astonishment, on the front of this age, so satisfied with itself, that in these days of progress and discovery, there was needed an iron law to forbid the murder of children by excessive labour.

This is language worthy of the compatriot of Massillon and Fenelon. It is the language of the primate of Normandy, uttered in the cathedral of Rouen, "that country of France," says M. Dupin, "in which the early labour of children has produced the greatest evils." Sir, I must say, from the bottom of my heart, that it is not a little agreeable, amid all our differences of opinion and religious strifes, to find one common point, on which we can feel a mutual sympathy, and join together in harmonious action. And now, Sir, to conclude this long, and, I fear, wearisome address—my first grand object, as I have already said, is to bring these children within the reach of education; it will then be time enough to fight about the mode. Only let us exhibit these evils—there is wit enough, experience enough, activity enough, and principle enough in the country, to devise some remedy. I am sure that the exhibition of the peril will terrify even the most sluggish, and the most reluctant, into some attempt at amendment; but I hope for far better motives. For my own part I will say, though possibly I may be charged with cant and hypocrisy, that I have been bold enough to undertake this task, because I must regard the objects of it as beings created, as ourselves, by the same Maker, redeemed by the same Saviour, and destined to the same immortality; and it is, therefore, in this spirit, and with these sentiments, which, I am sure, are participated by all who hear me; that I now venture to entreat the countenance of this House, and the co-operation of Her Majesty's Ministers; first to investigate, and ultimately to remove, these sad evils, which press so deeply and so extensively on such a large and such an interesting portion of the human race. I will, therefore, Sir, with very sincere thanks to the House, for the patience with which they have heard me now move,—

That an humble Address be presented to her Majesty, praying that her Majesty will be graciously pleased to direct an inquiry to be made into the employment of the children of the poorer classes in mines and collieries, and in the various branches of trade and manufacture in which numbers of children work together, not being included in the provisions of the acts for regulating the employment of children and young persons in mills and factories, and to collect information as to the ages at which they are employed, the number of hours they are engaged in work, the time allowed each day for meals, and as to the actual state, condition, and treatment of such children, and as to the effects of such employment, both with regard to their morals and their bodily health.

Mr. *Brotherton* seconded the motion. . . . Motion agreed to.

Seven

CORN LAW
RHYMES

Ebenezer Elliott

Ebenezer Elliott (1781-1849), "the corn-law rhymer," was originally in the iron trade in Sheffield. He gained the approbation of Robert Southey for his *Tales of the Night*. Elliott supported all of the popular movements of his day and for a
time was an ardent Chartist. He left the Chartists when they
did not participate in the anti-Corn Law movement.* Elliott
attributed all of the popular distress to the "bread tax," as he
designated the Corn Laws. He expressed his views in several
works, of which the most famous was *Corn-Law Rhymes*;
others were *The Ranter, The Village Patriarch,* and *The
Splendid Village*. Ebenezer Elliott cannot under any circumstances be thought of as a great poet, but in his day he was
very popular. His writings were widely read and much appre-
ciated, especially by the uneducated. Elliott has had the fate of
most authors of purely topical poetry: a certain popularity
during his life and almost total neglect by posterity. However,
it is necessary to see the literary as well as the political side
of the anti-Corn Law agitation to understand its impact. *Corn
Law Rhymes and Other Poems* (London, Benjamin Steuil,
1844).

---

* The first Corn Laws were passed in the reign of Charles II; they continued
to be enacted in various forms until 1815. The legislation of 1815—still in force
in 1845—aimed at keeping the price of grain (in Great Britain all grains are
called corn, and what is corn in the United States is called maize) at a level
which would ensure a good income for the landed classes. Grain could not be
imported until it had reached a set price per bushel. Increased free trade was
advocated in the 1820's on economic grounds, and again in the late 1830's as a
consequence of bad harvests. In 1839 the Anti-Corn Law League was established
in Manchester; the League was led by Cobden and Bright and turned into a
moral crusade against the bread-taxing oligarchy. The arguments of Cobden
and Bright in conjunction with the Irish famine caused Peel to abandon his
former protectionist position.

99

From The Corn Law Rhymes

Avenge the plunder'd poor, oh Lord!
But not with fire, but not with sword,
Not as at Peterloo they died,
Beneath the hoofs of coward pride.
Avenge our rags, our chains, our sighs,
The famine in our children's eyes!
But not with sword—no, not with fire
Chastise thou Britain's locustry!
Lord, let them feel thy heavier ire;
Whip them, oh Lord! with poverty!
Then, cold in soul as coffined dust,
Their hearts as tearless, dead and dry,
Let them in outraged mercy trust,
And find that mercy they deny!

Bread-tax eating absentee,
What hath bread-tax done for thee?—
Crammed thee from our children's plates,
Made thee all that nature hates,
Filled thy skin with untaxed wine,
Filled thy purse with cash of mine,
Filled thy breast with hellish schemes,
Filled thy head with fatal dreams
Of potatoes basely sold
At the price of wheat in gold,
And of Britons styed to eat
Wheat-priced roots instead of wheat.

England! what for mine and me,
What hath bread-tax done for thee?
It hath shown what kinglings are,
Stripp'd the hideous idols bare,
Sold thy greatness, stain'd thy name,
Struck thee from the rolls of fame.

Make haste, slow rogues! prohibit trade,
Prohibit honest gain;
Turn all the good that God hath made

To fear, and hate, and pain;
Till beggars all, assassins all,
All cannibals we be,
And death shall have no funeral,
From shipless sea to sea.

Child, what hast thou with sleep to do?
Awake, and dry thine eyes!
Thy tiny hands must labor too;
Our bread is taxed. Arise!
Arise, and toil long hours twice seven,
For pennies two or three;
Thy woes make angels weep in heaven,—
But England still is free.

Up, weary man of eighty-five,
And toil in hopeless woe!
Our bread is tax'd, our rivals thrive,
Our gods will have it so.
Yet God is undethroned on high,
And undethron'd be:
Father of all! hear thou our cry,
And England shall be free!

Eight

THE REPEAL OF
THE CORN LAWS

Sir Robert Peel

Sir Robert Peel (1788-1850), second baronet, great Victorian statesman and Tory prime minister, was elected to Parliament in 1807. He was associated with the liberal Tories. In his early career he was a leader in financial reforms—many of which foreshadowed his later free trade policy—and also in the repeal of the legislation against the Protestant Dissenters and the Roman Catholics. He was prime minister in 1834-1835 and again in 1841-1846. The disastrous harvest in Ireland in 1845 and the prospect of a famine convinced Peel that agricultural protection had to end. His Tory colleagues were not agreeable and Peel resigned, but upon the failure of the Whigs to form a government he reassumed office. The bill to end agricultural protection was introduced in January 1846 and Peel's speech of February 16, 1846, expounded most completely his and his followers' views on the question. It was perhaps the most carefully prepared statement on the consequences of the failure to establish free trade and the need to do so. The Corn Laws were repealed on 25 June, 1846; England was committed to free trade, but Peel had broken with his party and he retired from office. Peel's policies prevented violence and famine in Ireland, and ultimately his policy of free trade was to be considered one of the hallmarks of English prosperity in the Victorian age. "Sir Robert Peel's Speech on the Second Reading of the Bill for the Repeal of the Corn Laws, 16 February, 1846," *Hansard, 3rd Series,* Vol. LXXXIII (London, 1846).

Mr. Speaker, Two matters of great importance have occupied the attention of the House during this protracted debate—the one, the manner in which a party should be conducted; the other, the measures by which an imminent public calamity shall be mitigated, and the principles by which the commercial policy of a Great Empire shall for the future be governed. On the first point, the manner in which a party should be conducted, by far the greater part of this debate has turned. I do not undervalue its importance; but, great as it is, surely it is subordinate in the eyes of a people to that other question to which I have referred—the precautions to be taken against impending scarcity, and the principles by which your commercial policy shall hereafter be governed. On the party question I have little defence to make. Yes, Sir, these are I admit at once, the worst measures for party interests that could have been brought forward. I admit also that it is unfortunate that the conduct of this measure, so far as the Corn Laws are concerned, should be committed to my hands. It would, no doubt, have been far preferable, that those should have the credit, if credit there be, for an adjustment of the Corn Laws, who have been uniform and consistent opponents of those laws. That which prevented myself and those who concurred with me from committing it at once to other hands, was the firm conviction under which we laboured, that a part of this Empire was threatened with a great calamity.* I did firmly believe, I do firmly believe, that there is impending over you a calamity that all will deplore. I did think that while there was that danger, and while I had the hopes of averting it, it would not be consistent with my duty to my Sovereign, or with the honour of a public man, to take that opportunity of shrinking from the heavy responsibilities which it imposed. While I retained the hope of acting with a united Administration, while I thought there was a prospect of bringing this question to a settlement, I determined to retain office and incur its responsibili-

* This is a reference to the failure of the potato crop in Ireland in 1845; with the failure of the potato crop famine would follow because grain could not be imported into the country under the existing economic and agricultural protective legislation. Peel felt that the only answer was free trade which would allow the free importation of grain and thus avert the famine. Of Peel's conversion to repeal of the Corn Laws the Duke of Wellington supposedly said that it was the potatoes that put Peel into a damn fright.

ties. When I was compelled to abandon that hope (my sense of the coming evil remaining the same), I took the earliest opportunity, consistent with a sense of duty and of public honour, of tendering my resignation** to the Queen, and leaving Her Majesty the full opportunity of consulting other advisers. I offered no opinion as to the choice of a successor. That is almost the only act which is the personal act of the Sovereign; it is for the Sovereign to determine in whom Her confidence shall be placed. It was, indeed, my duty to ascertain, by the command of the Queen, whether those of my Colleagues who had dissented from me were either themselves prepared to form a Government, or to advise Her Majesty, if they themselves were not prepared, to commit to other hands the formation of a Government—a Government, I mean, to be composed of public men favourable to the maintenance of the existing Corn Law. Those from whom I differed, who had not concurred with me either as to the full extent of the danger to be apprehended, or as to the policy of altering the law, signified their opinion that it would not be for the public interests that they should form a Government; nor could they advise Her Majesty to resort to others for the formation of a Government founded on the maintenance of the existing Corn Law. Her Majesty determined to call upon the noble Lord (Lord J. Russell) to undertake the duty of forming an Administration. My firm belief was, that the noble Lord would have undertaken that duty; my firm persuasion was— the noble Lord will excuse me for saying so—that he would have succeeded if he had undertaken it. During the long course of my opposition to the noble Lord, I cannot charge myself with having ever said anything disrespectful of him. We have acted against each other for many years, and I don't recollect anything that ever passed between us likely to engender hostile or acrimonious feelings. But I must say, the noble Lord did disappoint me when he did not at once undertake the formation of a Government on the principle of adjusting this question. When my tender of resignation had been accepted, and when the noble Lord had been sent for by the Queen, I considered myself at perfect liberty to act in a private

---

**Peel resigned office December 6, 1845 and Queen Victoria asked Lord John Russell to form a government, but the Whig leader was unable to do so and Peel returned to office on December 20, 1845.

capacity on my own personal sense of the public interests, and my own feelings of public duty. I knew all the difficulties with which any man would have to contend who undertook the conduct of the Government. I knew there must be a great dislocation of parties. In the firm persuasion that the noble Lord would accept the office of First Minister, I felt it incumbent upon me, under the special circumstances under which he would have undertaken office, to diminish the difficulties with which he might have to contend in attempting a final settlement of the Corn Laws. I resolved, therefore, to give the noble Lord such assurances of support as it was in my power to give. In the explanation which I offered the other night, I limited myself to a detail of the facts which had preceded my retirement from office. The noble Lord's explanation commenced from that period. Of that explanation I have no complaint whatever to make. It was perfectly fair and candid on the part of the noble Lord. But there are additions to it which I am desirous of supplying, in the hope of being enabled to demonstrate that I had no wish to defraud others of the credit of adjusting the Corn Laws. My resignation of office was accepted by Her Majesty on the 6th of December last. On the 8th December, I addressed to Her Majesty the following communication, for the express purpose of enabling Her Majesty, by the knowledge of my views and intentions with regard to the Corn Laws, to diminish the difficulties of my successor:—

Whitehall, Dec. 8, 1845.

Sir Robert Peel presents his humble duty to Your Majesty, and, influenced by no other motive than the desire to contribute, if possible, to the relief of Your Majesty from embarrassment, and to the protection of the public interests from injury, is induced to make to Your Majesty this confidential communication explanatory of Sir Robert Peel's position and intentions with regard to the great question which is now agitating the public mind.

Your Majesty can, if you think fit, make this communication known to the Minister who, as successor to Sir Robert Peel, may be honoured by Your Majesty's confidence.

On the 1st of November last, Sir Robert Peel advised his Colleagues, on account of the alarming accounts from Ireland, and any districts in this country, as to the failure of the potato crop from disease, and for the purpose of guarding against contingencies, which in his opinion were not improbable, humbly to recommend to Your Majesty that the duties on the import of foreign grain should be suspended for a limited period, either by Order in Council or by Legislative Enactment; Parliament, in either case, being summoned without delay.

Sir Robert Peel foresaw that this suspension, fully justified by the tenor of the report to which he has referred, would compel, during the interval of suspension, the reconsideration of the Corn Laws.

If the opinions of his Colleagues had then been in concurrence with his own, he was fully prepared to take the responsibility of suspension— and of the necessary consequence of suspension, a comprehensive review of the laws imposing restrictions on the import of foreign grain and other articles of food, with a view to their gradual diminution and ultimate removal.

He was disposed to recommend that any new laws to be enacted should contain within themselves the principle of gradual reduction and final repeal.

Sir Robert Peel is prepared to support, in a private capacity, measures which may be in general conformity with those which he advised as a minister.

It would be unbecoming in Sir Robert Peel to make any reference to the details of such measures.

Your Majesty has been good enough to inform Sir Robert Peel that it is your intention to propose to Lord John Russell to undertake the formation of a Government.

The principle on which Sir Robert Peel was prepared to recommend the reconsideration of the laws affecting the import of the main articles of food was in general accordance with that referred to in the concluding paragraph of Lord John Russell's letter to the electors of the city of London.

Sir Robert Peel wished to accompany the removal of restriction on the admission of such articles with relief to the land from any charges that may be unduly onerous, and with such other provisions as, in the terms of Lord John Russell's letter, "caution and even scrupulous forbearance may suggest."

Sir Robert Peel will support measures founded on that general principle, and will exercise any influence he may possess to promote their success.

That was the assurance I conveyed to Her Majesty of my perfect readiness to support, if proposed by others, those measures which

I had myself deemed necessary. I could not but foresee that in addition to all the other difficulties with which the noble Lord or any other Minister would have to contend, there would be some connected with the state of our revenue and expenditure. At the close of the present financial year there will probably be, as there has been in the years preceding, a considerable surplus of revenue after providing for the wants of the public service. In the coming year there must be increased estimates, reducing the future surplus, and I thought it right that my successor should not be exposed to the risk of an unfavourable contrast for which he could not be responsible. I added, therefore, to my assurance of support with respect to the Corn Laws this further assurance. It refers to points of great delicacy, but it is better to have no concealment or reserve.

> Sir Robert Peel feels it to be his duty to add that, should Your Majesty's future advisers, after consideration of the heavy demands made upon the army of this country for colonial service, of our relations with the United States, and of the bearing which steam navigation may have upon maritime warfare and the defence of the country, deem it advisable to propose an addition to the army and increased naval and military estimates, Sir Robert Peel will support the proposal—will do all that he can to prevent it from being considered as indicative of hostile or altered feelings towards France, and will assume, for the increase in question, any degree of responsibility, present or retrospective, which can fairly attach to him.

Now, when it is charged on me, that I am robbing others of the credit which is justly due to them, I hope that this explanation of the course I pursued, when I was acting under the firmest persuasion that the adjustment of this question would be committed to others, may tend to prove that I was not desirous of robbing others of the credit of settling this question, or of trying to embarrass their course. There were further communications made, and in the course of those communications it was proposed to put me in possession of the particular mode in which the noble Lord intended to arrange this question. I thought that it would be better that I should not be made acquainted with such details. I thought that my knowledge of them, or any appearance of concert between the noble Lord and myself, would have had the tendency rather to

prejudice than promote the adjustment of this question. I, therefore, declined to receive the communication of those details; but
I think that the noble Lord must have been satisfied that, though
I declined to concert particular measures with him, yet it was my
intention to give to the noble Lord, in his attempt to adjust this
question according to his own views of public policy, that same
cordial support which it is his boast he now intends to give me.
I believe that must have been the impression of the noble Lord—
LORD J. RUSSELL: Hear, hear!)—because, after the communication with me, the noble Lord undertook the formation of a Government; and I am sure that the noble Lord will admit that no
act of mine caused the failure of the noble Lord's attempt, and
that I was in no way concerned in the reasons which induced the
noble Lord finally to abandon it. I made no inquiry as to the
persons who should constitute the new Government; I had no personal objections of any kind. My conviction was, that this question
ought to be adjusted. I was prepared to facilitate its adjustment by
others by my vote, and by the exercise of whatever influence I
could command. So much for my conduct towards political opponents—better entitled than myself to undertake the repeal of
the Corn Laws.

Now, Sir, with respect to the course which I have pursued towards those who so long have given me their support. I admit to
them that it is but natural that they should withhold from me their
confidence. I admit that the course which I am pursuing is at
variance with the principles on which party is ordinarily conducted. But I do ask of them, whether it be probable that I would
sacrifice their favourable opinion and their support unless I was
influenced by urgent considerations of public duty—unless I was
deeply impressed with the necessity of taking these precautions,
and advising these measures. Notwithstanding that which may have
passed in this debate—notwithstanding the asperity with which
some have spoken, I will do that party (which has hitherto supported me) the justice they deserve. No person can fill the situation
I fill without being aware of the motives by which a great party is
influenced. I must have an opportunity of knowing what are the
personal objects of those around me; and this I will say, notwithstanding the threatened forfeiture of their confidence, that I do

not believe (speaking generally of the great body of the party) that there ever existed a party influenced by more honourable and disinterested feelings.

While I admit that a natural consequence of the course I have pursued is to offend, probably to alienate, a great party, I am not the less convinced that any other course would have been ultimately injurious even to party interests. I know what would have conciliated temporary confidence. It would have been to underrate the danger in Ireland, to invite a united combination for the maintenance of the existing Corn Law, to talk about hoisting the flag of protection for native industry, to insist that agricultural protection should be maintained in all its integrity—by such a course I should have been sure to animate and please a party, and to gain for a time their cordial approbation. But the month of May will not arrive without demonstrating that I should thereby have abandoned my duty to my country—to my Sovereign—aye and to the Conservative party. I had, and have, the firm persuasion that the present temper of the public mind—the state of public feeling, and of public opinion, with respect to the Corn Laws—independent of all adventitious circumstances, make the defence of the Corn Laws a very difficult task. But with such a calamity as that which is impending in Ireland, it was utterly irreconcilable with my feelings to urge the landed interest to commit themselves to a conflict for the maintenance inviolate of a law which attaches at the present time a duty of 17s. to the quarter of wheat. What were the facts which came under the cognizance of my right hon. friend the Secretary of State for the Home Department, charged with the responsibility of providing for the public peace, and rescuing millions from the calamity of starvation? We were assured in one part of this Empire there are 4,000,000 of the Queen's subjects dependent on a certain article of food for subsistence. We knew that on that article of food no reliance could be placed. It was difficult to say what was the extent of the danger—what would be the progress of the disease, and what the amount of deficiency in the supply of the article of food. But, surely, you will make allowances for those who were charged with the heaviest responsibility, if their worst anticipations should be realized by the event. We saw, in the distance, the gaunt forms of famine, and of disease following in the train of famine. Was it not our duty to the country, aye, our duty to the party that supported us, to avert the odious charge of indifference and neglect of timely precautions? It is absolutely necessary, before you come to a final decision on this question, that you should understand this Irish case. You must do so. The reading of letters may be distasteful to you; but you shall have no ground for imputing it to me that I left you in ignorance of a danger which I believe to be imminent. I may have lost your confidence—I will not try to regain it at the expense of truth. I can conciliate no favour by the expression of regret for the course I have taken. So far from it, I declare, in the face of this House that the day of my public life, which I look back on with the greatest satisfaction and pride, is that 1st of November last, when I offered to take the responsibility of issuing an Order in Council to open the ports, and to trust to you for approval and indemnity. I wished then, that by the first packet which sailed after the 1st of November, the news might have gone forth that the ports were open. The primary object of such a measure, of course, would have been to increase the supply of food, and to take precautions against famine, although other collateral advantages might have flowed from it. Had we opened the ports, and had our anticipations proved to be incorrect—had the result shown that we had formed a false estimate of this danger—I believe that the generosity of Parliament would have protected us from censure. (Hear, hear.) That would have been the case had our anticipations proved to be wrong; but what is the fact? During the latter part of December and January, there was a temporary suspension of alarm, after the opinions we had received from men eminent in science. I never shared in the sanguine hopes that there would be abundance of food, that the potato disease was exaggerated, and that we might safely trust to existing supplies. I felt that the time would arrive when the opinions of those individuals would be justified. And what is the fact? I will read to you some communications, not so much for the vindication of the Government as for the guidance of your own future course. It is not right that I should leave you in ignorance of the real facts of this case. (Hear, hear.) It is true the present proposition is not a suspension of the duties, but it is a virtual suspension. It comprehends the removal of the duty on maize and rice, and the reduction of the duty to a nominal amount

on barley and oats, and the reduction of the duty on wheat from
17s. to 4s. Before you decide on rejecting or delaying this measure,
hear and consider the reports which the last few days have brought
from Ireland. You seemed to discredit the reports of official authorities; and some, I regret to say, countenanced the notion that public
men were base enough to act in concept for the purpose of exagger-
ation. I will now read, therefore, no reports from the Lord Lieutenant. I will read letters which the last two mails have brought from
Ireland, from men from whose statements you cannot have the
pretence of withholding confidence. I will first read a communication from Sir David Roche, who was for some time Member for
the city of Limerick. He was one of those who at first thought the
apprehension of famine to be greatly exaggerated, and that extraordinary precautions were unnecessary. This day has brought me
this letter from him, dated Carass, near Limerick, Feb. 11:—

> No person was more disposed than I was to look with hope to that part
> of the potato crop in this country that appeared sound before Christmas.
> I thought it was quite safe and certain to keep in the usual way, and in
> my answer to the Lord Lieutenant's circular I stated that hope with
> great confidence, adding that the crop was so large, the sound portion
> would nearly feed the people.

(This, then, is a disinterested authority.)

> But I grieve to say, that every day convinces me of the error I was
> under; the potatoes that were apparently sound then, had more or less
> the disease in an incipient state, and the greater part is now obliged to
> be given to pigs and cattle, to save the owners from total loss. The
> Catholic clergy of several parishes have made this painful communica-
> tion to me; my own experience as a landed proprietor and a practical
> farmer, holding in my possession large animal farms, in three different
> parts of this country, and also in the county Clare, entirely corresponds
> with their statements. I don't think by the 1st of May next, that out of
> one hundred acres of potatoes on my land, sound seed will be left me for
> next year's crop.
>   If the case is so bad with me, and it is nearly the same in the four
> districts I allude to, how much worse must it be with the poor, who
> have not the convenience and aid that large farming establishments,
> with substantial buildings, can command? In short, as one rides through

the country, rotten potatoes are to be seen everywhere in large quantities by the side of the roads; pits, lately turned, in most cases smaller than the heaps of rotten potatoes alongside them; and those in the pits are certain, if not quickly consumed, to share in the general decay.

Such, Sir, is the state I may say of the entire country. No doubt for six or seven weeks, while the remains of the potatoes last, destitution will not be general; but I pray you, Sir, look to it in time.

There were some of us who did look to it in time, and I wish that our advice had been acted on. That is the Report from the county of Limerick. I now come to the Queen's County. The following is a copy of a Report, received February 12, 1846:—

Queen's County, Stradbally, Feb. 11, 1846.

With reference to the potato disease, I beg to state that I was requested by Sir Edward Walsh and Sir A. Weldon, two magistrates of this district, to make a more searching inquiry into the state of the potatoes in the neighborhood of the collieries that had hitherto been made. The instructions were, to make the examination by properties, and ruled forms were supplied by Sir A. Weldon, with such headings as he considered applicable to the case.

On Monday morning, the 9th I proceeded to Wolfhill, accompanied by the Rev. Mr. Emerson, the clergyman of the parish, and commenced with the property of Mr. Hovenden. Mr. Hovenden himself being with us, we examined every house on the property, took down the number of each family, the quantity of potatoes planted, and the quantity (from actual inspection) now remaining on lands, with the quantity of oats or other grain now in the possession of the family. On Tuesday, we went over the property of Sir Charles Coote, adjoining Mr. Hovenden's, and also over Mr. Carter's, and so far as time would admit, examined a few families on the property of Mrs. Kavanagh, of Gracefield. Our inquires extended to about 190 families altogether, and enable me with the most perfect accuracy to state the frightful extent to which the destruction of the potato crop has proceeded in that part of the country. Many families whom we visited, and who had planted sufficient for their ordinary wants, including the seed necessary for the ensuing season, have not had a potato of any kind for the last month.

Observe this is in the month of February, five months at least before there can be any supply from the natural bounty of Providence.

Others have lost nearly all; and the few that still remain are totally unfit for human food. In every instance where we saw potatoes in pits in the fields we had them examined, and, with scarcely an exception, we found them to be a mass of putrefaction, perfectly disgusting, even to look at. We examined a few houses on the property of Sir Thomas Esmonde, where the land is of much better quality, but the result was in every case the same. There are literally no potatoes remaining in that part of the country.

I understand the magistrates intend to meet on an early day, and make some representation, through the lieutenant of the county, on the above subject.

W. W. HEMSWORTH,
Sub-Inspector 1st Rate.

I pass on to Waterford. There are letters received within the last two days; one from the Lord Lieutenant of that county—Lord Stuart de Decies. It is dated the 10th February; I entreat the attention of the House to it. Lord Stuart de Decies is a person whose opinions must carry with them great authority. He says—

His excellency will find in these statements an announcement of the alarming fact, that in two districts alone of the Union in question there are even at this early period of the year, no less than 300 persons whose stores of provisions are upon the point of becoming exhausted. In the meanwhile the rot is represented as making daily progress amongst the potatoes, which until lately it was hoped might have been preserved in a state of partial soundness for some time longer; and there is every reason, therefore, to anticipate that the distress now prevailing in certain localities will very speedily cause its pressure to be felt by the labouring classes throughout the Union. With this prospect in view, the probability is, that a rise in the price of all kinds of grain may be expected to take place in the course of the ensuing spring and summer months, although foreign supplies were to be admitted immediately duty free, and thus the facilities of providing food for the people in exchange for their labour be removed beyond the means which landed proprietors have at the present moment within their reach for this purpose. It is in these circumstances that I would venture respectfully to submit, as far as the interests of the county of Waterford are involved, that much good might be effected in keeping down prices by the establishment of Government corn stores from which grain might be purchased at first cost price in such towns as Youghal, Dungarvan, Water-

ford, Carrick, Clonmel, and, perhaps, Lismore. In all but the last mentioned of these towns, there is an adequate military force for the protection of such granaries, if established, and no part of the county would
then be beyond twelve or fourteen miles distance from a depot, whence
food on moderate terms might be drawn to those localities which stood
in need of a supply.

The next I read is from Kerry, dated the 9th of February, from a
gentleman whose statements I believe are entitled to the highest
respect—Mr. Thomas Dillon:—

> I regret to have to report, for the information of Government, that
> serious ravages have been made latterly on the potatoes by the disease
> which, for the last two months, was supposed at least not to be progres-
> sive. Having gone round my district within the last ten days, I have had
> opportunities not only of hearing, but of witnessing the destruction
> which has been committed, and which is gaining ground rapidly, con-
> trary to the hopes which have been for some time cherished, as to excite
> the utmost alarm among all classes: and for my own part I feel almost
> confounded at the difficulty that must exist in procuring a sufficiency of
> good seed for the ensuing crop.

Such is the report of Mr. Dillon, of Cahirciveen, resident magis-
trate. The House is aware that there has been sitting for some time
past in Dublin a Commission, one of whose duties it has been to
collect accurate information with respect to the extent of the
deficiency in different localities. That Commission has lately made
a report, which refers, I fear, to a period antecedent to that in
which the disease has reappeared. I have here an official statement,
from the highest authority, embracing almost every part of Ireland,
every electoral district, with the exception of ninety-nine, having
sent returns; and these are the facts reported by the Commissioners:—

> That in four electoral divisions the loss of potatoes has been nearly
> nine-tenths of the whole crop; in 93, between seven-tenths and eight-
> tenths; in 125, the loss approaches to seven-tenths of the whole crop;
> in 16, it approaches to six-tenths; in 596, nearly one-half of tne crop is
> entirely destroyed; and in 582 divisions, nearly four-tenths of the crop
> are entirely destroyed.

Here are requisitions made to us, and we are acting upon them, to establish stores of corn for the people, to be retailed at cost prices, or given in remuneration for labour. (An hon. Member: It will be wanted for seed.) Yes; to get potatoes from foreign countries for the ensuing year is next to impossible. An eighth of the whole crop is required for seed; each acre of potatoes requires nearly a ton, three-fourths of a ton, at least, for seed; take the tonnage which it would require to bring in 10,000 tons of potatoes from any part of Europe where potatoes may still abound; it is impossible to supply the deficiency by foreign import. You must look for seed from the domestic supply—by making savings from the existing crop. And here is the danger, that when the pressure of famine is severe, the immediate craving of hunger will be supplied—the necessities of next year will be forgotten; the Government must interfere for the purpose of encouraging the saving of potatoes in sufficient quantities, in order to secure a supply of seed for next year. How are we to do this? By the substitution, I suppose, of some other articles of provision, to be given under wise regulations, for the purpose of preventing abuse. Suppose, now, that in April or May next, we shall be under the necessity of proposing votes of public money to cover past or future expenditure—will there be a cheerful acquiescence in those votes, if the Corn Law is to remain unaltered? We are now encouraging the resident proprietors, the clergy of the Established Church, and the clergy of the Roman Catholic persuasion, to make great exertions; we are telling them, "Individual charity in your localities must supply more than the Government can supply; you must give corn in exchange for seed potatoes, or for the sustenance of human life." Is it quite reasonable to make these demands on the private charity of those whose straitened means leave little disposable for charity, and at the same time to levy 17s. duty on the quarter of foreign wheat? Is the State to show no charity? For what is the duty to be levied? For Revenue? But we may have to spend public money in the purchase of corn— we may have to raise its price to the consumer by our unusual intervention. Surely it is a more becoming course to remit duty, than to buy heavily taxed corn! Shall we levy the 17s. for protection to domestic corn? What—when in 600 electoral divisions in Ireland only half the crop of potatoes has been saved, and in 600 more only three-fifths, while in some, nearly eight-tenths are gone? Do you believe that it would be for the credit and honour of the landed aristocracy of this country to say, "We throw upon the Government the responsibility of averting the evils of famine, but not one letter of the existing Corn Law shall be altered?" Would it be fidelity to the landed interest were I to counsel this? No; I believe that, whatever might have been the outward show of consistency, such a proposal would be the real "treachery" which you impute to me, because I have thought it for your interest, and the interests of all, to relieve ourselves from the odium of stipulating for these restrictions on food in such a moment of pressure. What would have been said? Why, the pressure in Holland and in Belgium is not half so severe as it will be in Ireland; and see what the Government in those two countries did at an early period of the autumn. In Belgium, the Executive Government took upon itself the responsibility of opening the ports to every description of provisions. The Government of Holland exercised the power which it had to do this by ordinance. Belgium is an agricultural country; the Chambers (the Lords and Commons of a neighbouring State) assembled; the Government asked for indemnity, and for the continuance of open ports. Without a moment's hesitation, by acclamation as it were, without one dissentient voice, the representatives of the landed interest in Belgium gave the Government indemnity, and continued the permission freely to import every article of food. What, under similar circumstances, has been the course taken by the Parliament of this country? What has been the course taken by Parliaments as deeply interested as we can be in the welfare of agriculture? There have been times before the present when there has been the apprehension of scarcity in this country; what has been the remedy? What has been the remedy that the heart of every man suggested? What has been the remedy that legislative wisdom took? Why, in every case, without exception, the removal for a time of the duties upon foreign corn. (Cheers.) (An hon. Member: What was done at the end of the time?) I will come to that immediately. I rejoice in the cheer which I received from that quarter (looking to the Protection benches); what is it but an assent—apparently a unanimous assent—("No!") at any rate, a very general assent—that at a period of impending famine, the proper precaution to be taken is to encourage the free importation of food? I have a right to infer, that if that had been the proposal, namely, that existing duties upon corn and other articles of provision should be suspended for a time that proposal would have met with general assent. Then, if that be so, I ask you to expedite the passing of this Bill: either do that, or move as an Amendment that the duties upon all articles of provision shall forthwith be suspended.

I will not omit the other consideration—the course to be taken after you have suspended the law; I am trying now to convince you that I should have been unfaithful and treacherous to the landed interest, and to the party that protect the landed interest, if I had concealed the real pressure of this Irish case, and had called forth party cheers by talking about "hoisting the flag of protection"—or "rousing the British lion"—or "adhering to the true blue colour"—or steadfast maintenance of the Corn Laws "in all their integrity." I am trying to convince you, by fair reasoning, that that is a course which would not have been consistent either with the public interest, or with the credit of the landed aristocracy. That is all I am asking you now to admit. If you answer me, "We will readily consent to suspend this law until next harvest," I am rejoiced to have that admission from three-fourths of those by whom I shall be opposed, that it would but be wise to stipulate that for the present no alteration should be made in the Corn Law, that no maize should be admitted, at a reduced rate of duty, and that the duty upon wheat should be maintained at 17s.; I am rejoiced that I have established, to the satisfaction of the great majority, that that would not have been a prudent or a defensible course, I say it would not, because at all periods of our history the natural precaution that has been taken has been the admission, free of duty, of foreign corn in times of scarcity. I must quote some of those instances. In 1756, there was the apprehension of famine: Parliament was assembled: the first step taken was to prohibit, unwisely, in my opinion, the exportation of corn; the second was, to permit importation duty free. In 1767, you were again threatened with scarcity: the first act of the Parliament was, to admit provisions duty free. In 1791, Parliament altered the Corn Laws—they established a new Corn Law; in 1793, there was the apprehension of scarcity; notwithstanding the new Corn Law, one of the very first

Acts upon the Statute Book of 1793 is to remove, for a time, all duties upon the importation of foreign corn. In 1795, there was an apprehension, not of famine, but of scarcity, severely pressing upon some classes of the community; and in that year, and again in 1796, the same remedy was adopted—the removal of all duty upon foreign corn. In 1799, the same course was pursued, and free importation allowed. Why then, I ask, with all these precedents—when the danger, in the case of some at least, was less than it is at present—would it have been wise for a Government to counsel that we should pursue a different course, refuse facilities for importation, and determine upon maintaining the existing law? Sir, I believe that course would have involved the Government and the Parliament in the greatest discredit; and so far from assisting us in maintaining the existing law, my firm belief is, that that law would have been encumbered with a degree of odium which would have made the defence of it impossible. It was upon these grounds that I acted. Seeing what had been done in neighbouring countries, and what had been uniformly done by your own Parliament, not when corn was at 100s. or 80s., but in periods when it was under 60s.—seeing that the acknowledged remedy for scarcity was opening the ports for the admission of foreign corn, I advised the suspension of the Corn Laws. Do not answer me by saying, "There was at the period to which you refer, a different Corn Law—there was no sliding-scale—there was no admission of foreign corn at a low duty when the price was high." It was exactly the reverse of this; during the whole of that period, when corn was above 54s. in price, it was admitted at a duty of 6d.; the law made provision for the free importation of corn with even moderate prices. And why did Parliament interfere? It was in order that the high duty should not attach on a reduction of price. When corn was below 54s., there was a duty of from 2s. 6d. to 24s. 3d.; when it was above 54s., the duty was 6d.; by the natural operation of the law, therefore, corn was admitted when prices were high; but there was a fear that, from a sudden importation from neighbouring ports, corn might fall below 54s., and the high duty might attach. To prevent that, and to give a guarantee to the foreign importer that he should be certain for a period of six months to have his corn admitted at a duty of 6d., Parliament interposed, and gave him that guarantee. If, then, we had refused to interfere, what a contrast might have been drawn between us and those Parliaments! Would refusal have been, or would it now be, for the credit either of Parliament or of Government? I think not. We advised, therefore—at least I advised, and three of my Colleagues concurred with me— the immediate suspension of the law. The question is, what shall we do now? The law is not suspended—Parliament is sitting. It would be disrespectful towards Parliament for the Executive to take any step; it is impossible for the Executive, by an Order of Council, to do that which might have been done by an extreme exercise of authority, when Parliament was not sitting; it would not be constitutional to do it. It may be true that the best time has passed away; that the 1st of November was a better period for doing this than the present. Yes, but admitting that the necessity for acting with decision on the 16th February is only increased. True, the supplies of foreign corn might have been more ample had the ports been opened on the 1st November; but you have six months yet before you—and what course do you suggest? If any one dissents from that course which we propose, let him propose another. You must make your choice. You must either maintain the existing law, or make some proposal for increasing the facilities of procuring foreign articles of food.

And now I come to that second consideration from which I said I would not shrink. After the suspension of the existing law, and the admission of foreign importation for a period of several months, how do you propose to deal with the existing Corn Laws? That is the question which a Minister was bound to consider who advised the suspension of the Corn Laws. Now, my conviction is so strong that it would be utterly impossible, after establishing perfect freedom of trade in corn for a period of seven or eight months, to give a guarantee that the existing Corn Law should come into operation at the end of that period, that I could not encourage the delusive hope of such a result. I know it may be said, that after a temporary suspension of the law, the law itself would revive by its own operation, that there would be no necessity for any special enactment to restore its vigour. But I think it is an utter misapprehension of the state of public opinion to suppose it possible that after this country, for eight months, should have tasted of freedom in the trade in corn, you could revive, either by the tacit operation of the law itself, or by new and special enactment, the existing Corn Law. Surely, the fact of suspension would be a condemnation of the law. It would demonstrate that the law, which professed by the total reduction of duty on corn when it had reached a certain price to provide security against scarcity, has failed in one of its essential parts. Yet you insist on the revival of this law. Now let me ask, would you revive the existing Corn Law in all its provisions? Would you refuse the admission of maize at lower duties? —at present the duty on maize is almost prohibitory. Do not suppose that those who advised suspension overlooked the consideration of the consequences of suspension—of the bearing it would have upon the state of the Corn Laws, and the question of future protection. At the expiration of suspension will you revive the existing law, or will you propose a new and modified Corn Law? If the existing law, every manifest defect must be preserved. By that law, the duty on maize varies inversely not with the price of maize, but with the price of barley. We want maize—the price of barley is falling, but we can get no maize, because there is a prohibitory duty on maize in consequence of the low price of barley. Oh, say some, we will have a little alteration of the law, we will provide for the case of maize. Now, do not disregard public feeling in matters of this kind. It is not right that mere feeling should overbear the deliberate conviction of reason; but depend upon it, that when questions of food are concerned, public feeling cannot safely be disregarded. In the course of last Session notice was given that maize should be imported duty free, because it was for the interest of the farmer to have maize for food for cattle. Do you think it possible to devise a new Corn Law, the leading principle of which should be that maize should come in duty free, because the admission of that article would enable the farmer to feed his cattle and pigs with it, but that there are certain other articles used for consumption by human beings—and in respect to them the law shall be maintained in all its force? Do you advise me to commit you to fight that battle? I am assuming now that the necessity for the suspension of the law has been established; that suspension having taken place, would you deliberately advise the Government, for the sake of the public interests, or for the sake of party interests, to give a pledge either that the existing Corn Law, at the expiration of that suspension should be revived unaltered—or that there should be some trumpery modification of it, for the special benefit of the feeders of pigs and cattle? Are you insensible to the real state of public opinion on this question? Are you insensible to the altered convictions of many of your own party? Could I safely rely upon your cordial and unanimous support, as a party, for the redemption of that pledge? Look to the change of opinion, not among politicians, which you are apt to attribute to some interested or corrupt motives; but look to the opinions that have been expressed—to the sincerity of which conclusive proofs have been given by some of the most honourable men that ever sat upon these benches. Did my noble friend Lord Ashley vacate his seat for the county of Dorset from any interested or corrupt motive? Did Mr. Sturt, or Mr. W. Patten, avow their change of opinion from any interested or corrupt motives? Did Mr. Tatton Egerton offer to vacate his seat for Cheshire, or Lord Henniker his seat for Suffolk, from any other than a real change of opinion—from a conviction that the time was come for the adjustment of the question of the Corn Laws? Did Mr. Dawnay vacate his seat from such motive? Did a young Member of this House, Mr. Charteris, glowing with as high and honourable a spirit as ever animated the breast of an English gentleman—distinguished for great acuteness—great intelligence—great promise of future eminence—did he abandon his seat for Gloucestershire, and withdraw from this stirring conflict from any interested or corrupt motives? Surely these are proofs that that Minister who should suspend the law, and give a guarantee of the revival of it when the period of suspension expired, would have enormous difficulties to contend with.

But let us observe the course of the present debate, the admission and expressions of opinion of those who have been loudest in their condemnation of the Government. The first I notice is the hon. Member for Huntingdon. Well, I confess I was surprised to hear from a gentleman of the name of Baring, some of the opinions introduced by him in regard to commerce and the Corn Laws. Would that hon. Gentleman follow me in the maintenance of the existing Corn Law after the suspension of it? So far from it, the hon. Gentleman thinks that this is just the time for a compromise on the subject. He then would abandon me, if, after the suspension, I had undertaken a guarantee to revive the existing law. He says this is just the time for a compromise. If ever there was an unfortunate moment for a compromise, it is the present. What is the meaning of a compromise? Clearly, a new Corn Law. Now, what would be the security for the permanence of that new Corn Law? (Cheers from the Protection benches.) You cheer; but what says every hon. Gentleman who has appeared on the part of the agriculturists? That what the agriculturist chiefly wishes for is permanence as to the Corn Law. Would a modified Corn Law give that assurance of permanence? Is there, in truth, any choice between maintenance of the existing Corn Law and its repeal? . . .

This night, then—if on this night the debate shall close—you will have to decide what are the principles by which your commercial policy is to be regulated. Most earnestly, from a deep conviction, founded not upon the limited experience of three years alone, but upon the experience of the results of every relaxation of restriction and prohibition, I counsel you to set the example of liberality to other countries. Act thus, and it will be in perfect consistency with the course you have hitherto taken. Act thus, and you will provide an additional guarantee for the continued contentment, and happiness, and well-being of the great body of the people. Act thus, and you will have done whatever human sagacity can do for the promotion of commercial prosperity.

You may fail. Your precautions may be unavailing. They may give no certain assurance that mercantile and manufacturing prosperity will continue without interruption. It seems to be incident to great prosperity that there shall be a reverse—that the time of depression shall follow the season of excitement and success. That time of depression must perhaps return; and its return may be coincident with scarcity caused by unfavourable seasons. Gloomy winters, like those of 1841 and 1842, may again set in. Are those winters effaced from your memory? From mine they never can be. Surely you cannot have forgotten with what earnestness and sincerity you re-echoed the deep feelings of a gracious Queen, when at the opening and at the close of each Session, She expressed the warmest sympathy with the sufferings of Her people, and the warmest admiration of their heroic fortitude.

These sad times may recur. "The years of plenteousness may have ended," and "the years of dearth may have come"; and again you may have to offer the unavailing expressions of sympathy, and the urgent exhortations to patient resignation.

Commune with your own hearts and answer me this question: will your assurances of sympathy be less consolatory—will your exhortations to patience be less impressive—if, with your willing consent, the Corn Laws shall have then ceased to exist? Will it be no satisfaction to you to reflect, that by your own act, you have been relieved from the grievous responsibility of regulating the supply of food? Will you not then cherish with delight the reflection that, in this the present hour of comparative prosperity, yielding to no clamour, impelled by no fear—except, indeed, that provident fear, which is the mother of safety—you had anticipated the evil day, and, long before its advent, had trampled on every impediment to the free circulation of the Creator's bounty?

When you are again exhorting a suffering people to fortitude under their privations, when you are telling them, "These are the chastenings of an all-wise and merciful Providence, sent for some inscrutable but just and beneficial purpose—it may be, to humble our pride, or to punish our unfaithfulness, or to impress us with the sense of our own nothingness and dependence on His mercy," when you are thus addressing your suffering fellow subjects, and encouraging them to bear without repining the dispensations of Providence, may God grant that by your decision of this night you may have laid in store for yourselves the consolation of reflecting that such calamities are, in truth, the dispensations of Providence—that they have not been caused, they have not been aggravated by laws of man restricting, in the hour of scarcity, the supply of food!

Nine

THE NEED FOR
IMPROVED EDUCATION

Richard Cobden

Richard Cobden (1804-1865), liberal statesman and humanitarian, was one of the founders of the Anti-Corn Law League.
He was a member of Parliament from 1841-1857 and 1859-
1864. In 1860 he negotiated the famous commercial treaty or
"Cobden Treaty" with France. Cobden was interested in all
forms of liberalism and he was opposed to tyranny in any
form. He was a champion of the dissenting interest against
the educational monopoly of the Church of England, and was
active in the National Education Movement. In January 1851
a great conference was held in Manchester. In his speech at
this conference Cobden advocated what was then called "The
Massachusetts System," which provided for free, compulsory,
and secular education. The reformers were not immediately
successful—indeed Cobden's proposals were not enacted
until 1870. But his work started a movement which ultimately
led to public education in England—education controlled by
the state and not by any religious body—which added to the
democratization of the country. "Education, Manchester, 22
January, 1851," *Speeches by Richard Cobden* (London, Mac-
millan & Co., 1903).

The aspect of this room certainly affords encouragement
to the friends of Education. The very numerous and influential
body of gentlemen that I see before me is a proof of the growing
interest taken in this important question; and I see around me
many gentlemen,—I see many of the old familiar faces with whom

I was associated in a former struggle*; and if continuous courage and perseverance, and an undeviating adherence to principle under trying circumstances can warrant success, then, I think, the past experience which those gentlemen have given to the world, augurs a triumph for the cause we have now in hand. But, gentlemen, I don't disguise from myself,—and you will not for a moment conceal from your minds, that we are indebted for this meeting, in some degree, to a recent movement that has taken place in this city by gentlemen who have hitherto not taken a prominent part in the cause of national education.

Now I join most unfeignedly in the expression of congratulation upon the fact that those gentlemen have come forward to avow, to a great extent, their adhesion to the principles of this association. They have given the sanction of their approval to the main features of this association, as has been well observed,—they have adopted the principles of local rating; and I will further say, they have, by one of the provisions of that scheme which has been published to the world, given in their adhesion to the principle of secular education, inasmuch as they leave to the parents of children the power of demanding for their children an exemption from that doctrinal instruction which has been hitherto held by every party an indispensable requisite of education. Now, I must confess, I have always been so impressed with the difficulties of this question, that if a proposal had been made by which it was intended to give an improved education to the people, coupled with conditions ten times as objectionable as those we have lately had proposed to us, I do not think I could have found it in my heart to have offered any very strong opposition. I have really passed beyond the time in which I can offer any opposition to any scheme whatever, come from whatever party it may, which proposes to give the mass of the people of this country a better education than they now receive. I will say more,—that in joining the secular system of education, I have not taken up the plan from any original love for a system of education which either separates itself from religion, or which sets up some peculiar and novel model of a system which shall be different from anything which has preceded it in

* The repeal of the Corn Laws; Richard Cobden had been closely associated with John Bright in the Anti-Corn Law League. [Ed. note.]

this country. I confess that for fifteen years my efforts in education, and my hopes of success in establishing a system of national education, have always been associated with the idea of coupling the education of this country with the religious communities which exist. But I have found, after trying it, as I think, in every possible shape, such insuperable difficulties in consequence of the religious discordances of this country,—that I have taken refuge in this, which has been called the remote haven of refuge for the Educationists,— the secular system,—in sheer despair of carrying out any system in connection with religion. I should, therefore, be a hypocrite, if I were to say I have any particular repugnance to a system of education coupled with religious instruction. But there is no one in this room, or in the country, that can have a stronger conviction than I have of the utter hopelessness of ever attempting to unite the religious bodies of this country in any system of education; so that I can hardly bring myself even to give a serious consideration to the plan that has been now brought forward by gentlemen in this city, and who have brought it forward, no doubt, with the best possible intentions, and who have only to persevere in order to find what I have found, for the last fifteen years,—the hopelessness of the task. For what is it those gentlemen have now proposed to do? Is there any novelty in it? Why, it is precisely what Parliament, and the Government, and the Committee of Privy Council, have been attempting to do now for a great number of years,—that is, to give a system of education to the country which shall comprise religious instruction, and which shall call upon the people of this country to subscribe, through taxation or rates, for the general religious as well as secular education of the country.

There is no novelty in the plan now brought forward; it is merely a proposal to transfer to Manchester, as the theatre of contest, what has been hitherto just going on in the House of Commons and the Government. It is, in fact, a proposal by which everybody shall be called upon to pay for the religious teaching of everybody else. Now, this is precisely what has been objected to by a great portion of this community, and what has prevented the present system, administered through the Minutes of Council, from being successful. There is this novelty, certainly,—that for the first time a body of Churchmen have themselves come forward, and recommended that all religious denominations should be allowed to receive public money for the teaching of their catechisms and creeds. Now, that is a novelty, because hitherto although the Church body have themselves been in favour of endowment for one particular sect,—if I may be allowed to call it so,—yet the Church has not hitherto been an active promoter of any system which shall recognise the right of other religious sects to receive public money to teach their catechisms. So far, then, we have a difference in the quarter from which this proposal has come; but does this alter the character of the opposition we may expect from those who have hitherto opposed the Minutes of Council and the parliamentary grants for education? It is precisely the same thing over again,—the same thing, whether you ask the religious voluntaries of this country to receive and pay public money for religious teaching through a local rate in Manchester, or through the Minutes in Council voted by Parliament in the annual grants. There is no difference in the two proposals, except that one is done by rates levied in Manchester, and the other by a vote in the House of Commons. How then are we to escape those difficulties in the religious question which we have hitherto encountered? If the members of the dissenting bodies have been sincere in their opposition hitherto to the national system of education, as administered through the Minutes of the Committee of Privy Council, there is not the slightest hope of that proposal, which has now emanated from the Church party in Manchester, being acceptable to this city. But I am not sure we are dealing with any well-considered or matured proposition from any particular religious body. We probably have the plan of an individual rather than the manifesto of a party. I am not sure that any party in this city, any religious body as a body, or any committee as a committee, has yet endorsed the proposal submitted to us; and I do not think the gentlemen who have so far given in their adhesion to this proposal, as to assemble together and discuss it, have considered the ultimate bearing and scope of the proposal that has been put forward. It is based upon the principle of voting public money for the teaching of the religious creeds of every religious denomination in the country. If it does not recognise that principle, it is an unjust proposal. There are but two principles on which you can carry on an education system in this country, or in any other, with the slightest approximation to justice. The one is, if you will have a religion, to form your plan so as to pay for the teaching of all religions; the other is, to adopt the secular system, and leave religion to voluntary effort.

Now, I must say, I doubt if the gentlemen who have so far joined this new association as to attend in person to hear it mooted,—I question if they fully understand the ultimate scope of what must be their proposal, if carried out with fairness; for it amounts to this, that you should pay from the public rates of this city the money for educating children in the Church schools, where, independent of the secular education which they shall have secured to them, they shall be taught the Church Catechism; and to the Independents, the Baptists, and the Unitarians and Wesleyans, the same system would be applied, in which, besides the secular instruction which should be enforced, they must be allowed to teach their various creeds or catechisms. But there is a large body in Manchester and Salford lying at the very lowest stratum of society, whose education must be embraced in any plan, or that plan must be worse than a mere pretence, fraught with downright injustice and negligence, and negligence of the most necessitous portion of the people. I speak of the Roman Catholics,—that portion of the people which was described by Dr. Kay, now Sir James Shuttleworth, in his pamphlet written here, some fourteen years ago,—that portion of the population which he has described, comprising 60,000 or 80,000 of the Irish, or immediate descendants of the Irish, being all Roman Catholics, and who import into this city a great deal of that barbarism which has, unfortunately, characterised the country from which they came. Any system which does not embrace that part of the population, cannot be entertained for a moment as a system.

Well, then, the proposal of the Church party must mean, that the schooling of all of those Roman Catholic children shall be paid out of the public rates, and that, besides the secular instruction they may receive, they shall be taught their catechism, and be permitted to observe their other religious ceremonies, precisely in the same way that the Church of England and the dissenting schools are allowed to do. Have those gentlemen made up their minds that they will pay rates for the purpose of the religious training of the

Roman Catholic children? Now, I say, I should be a hypocrite if I expressed any great repugnance myself to that which would give these poor children an education, coupled with that sort of instruction which I am here to advocate. But have the gentlemen who put forward this proposal fully considered the scope of their own plan? Have they made up their minds that the whole of the Roman Catholic children in Manchester shall be taught their religion at the expense of the rate-payers of Manchester? Have they made up their minds, when they talk of enforcing the reading of the Bible— have they made up their minds what version of the Bible they mean in all this? Has that subject been discussed among them,— has it been settled? Do they mean that the Douay version of the Bible shall be taught in these Roman Catholic schools? Because, if they do not mean that, when they make the Bible the condition of receiving any schooling, it is at once shutting the door most effectually to the instruction of the great mass of the Roman Catholic children in this town. Do not let any one suppose I am interposing these objections as my objections. They are what I have encountered here for the last fifteen years. I remember so long ago as 1836, when Mr. Wyse, himself a Roman Catholic, and Mr. Simpson, of Edinburgh, and others, came down here to enlighten us on the subject of education—I remember having in my counting-house in Mosley Street, the ministers of religion of every denomination, and trying to bring them to some sort of agreement on the system of education we were then anxious to advocate. I believe the insuperable difficulties that then existed have even increased now, and have not been in the slightest degree modified; and I believe those gentlemen who, with the best intentions, have brought forward this plan now, will find, before they have pursued it to one-twentieth part of the time and trouble gentlemen here have given to the Education question, that they have attempted an impossibility, and will be compelled to turn aside from what they are attempting to do. And if they view education at all as of that paramount importance I trust they do, the effect of this well-meant effort will be to bring many of those gentlemen to our ranks, if, as I sincerely hope and trust will be the case, we do nothing in the meantime to repel them from joining us.

The difficulties I spoke of have been encountered in two other countries, the most resembling us in the state of their civilisation and religion—the United States and Holland. They have both gone through the very same ordeal. In the United States, the education was once religious. When the Pilgrim Fathers landed in New England, the system of education then commenced embraced religious teaching; everybody was taught the Catechism, and there was no objection made to it. But when the number of sects multiplied, this religious education became a bone of contention; a great struggle ensued, and the Americans have had to go through the same difficulty that we have now; and it has ended, as it will end in this case, in the fundamental principle laid down in the Massachusetts statute for erecting common schools, which says that no book shall be admitted in the schools, and nothing taught, which favours the peculiar doctrines of any particular religious sect. In Holland, they have come to precisely the same conclusion. There they have adopted a system of secular education, because they have found it impracticable to unite the religious bodies in any system of combined religious instruction.

Well, now, if ever there was a time when it was desirable, more than another, to try and separate religious from secular instruction, it is the present time. And why? Because we have arrived at that period when all the world is agreed that secular instruction is a good thing for society. There are no dissentients now, or, if there be, they dare not avow themselves. We are agreed that it is good that English boys and girls shall be taught to read, and write, and spell, and should get as much grammar and geography as they can possibly imbibe. There is no difference of opinion about putting the elements of knowledge into the minds of every child in the land, if it can be done. But while we are all united on that, can any one who moves in society conceal from himself that we are also arrived at a time when we have probably more religious discord impending over us than at any period of our history? I do not allude to the dissensions between Roman Catholics and Protestants; I do not allude to them, excepting so far as they may lead to schisms and controversies in the internal state of other religious bodies. But I think there is at the present moment looming in the distance, and not in the very remote distance, a schism of the Church of England itself. I think you have two parties, one probably more

strong than the other in numbers, but the other far more strong
in intellect and logic, which are going to divide the Church. I see
the Wesleyan body torn asunder by a schism, which, I think, the
most sanguine can hardly hope to see healed; and I think there
are several other religious bodies, not perfectly tranquil in their
religious organisation.

Now, while we have the prospect of these great internal dissensions in religious bodies,—while we are all agreed that secular
education is a good thing,—is it desirable, if it can be avoided—
would it be desirable, if it were practicable, which it is not, I
think,—that our national education should be one which is united
and bound up with the religious organisations, when schisms may
prevail in the churches, and must be necessarily transferred with
increased virulence to the schools? For bear in mind that what you
see now pervading the churches in Scotland, where you have an
irreconcilable dispute with regard to the appointment of the masters
of the parochial schools—a dispute between the Old Kirk and the
Free Church—recollect, if what I say be correct, that you have an
impending schism in the Anglican Church, that then you will have
precisely the same difficulty in the appointment of masters in the
national schools. You will have High and Low Church contending
for the appointment of masters; in one parish, High Church pre-
dominating, the masters will be dwelling on the necessity of the
old forms of the Church, and enforcing the ritual and observance
prescribed by the Liturgy and Canons; and in another you will
have the Low Church, on the other hand, dwelling on what they
regard as the more vital essence of religion, and discountenancing
those forms which the High Church regard; and you will have the
same discords pervading your schools; and the consequence will
be, decreased efficiency of the masters, and, in some cases, a divided
school, a disruption of the school along with the congregation;
and you will have to fight the battle again, to reconcile the different
bodies; and in the end, I believe in my conscience, it will come
as in America and Holland to this,—you will be obliged, after a
great waste of time, to return to the secular system which they have
adopted, and which we are met here to advocate.

Since I addressed you here last, I have been visiting many places
—Birmingham, Leeds, Huddersfield, Bolton, and elsewhere,—and

I have sought private interviews with numerous bodies of gentle-men interested in the question. I have especially sought private interviews with those who have been supposed to differ from us, but have been thought usually as ardent advocates of education as our-selves,—those connected with the dissenting bodies in different parts of the kingdom. I have endeavoured to meet them privately, and to have a full and free discussion of the question, because I thought that such a cause would be more likely to put them in possession of the real objects of this association, which have been so much misunderstood. I thought it better to do so in a private conference, rather than to enter on an antagonistic discussion with them in the public arena, where they might be committed to views which I hope and trust, when they have fully considered our plan, they may be induced to modify and even to change. One of the objec-tions made to our plan has been alluded to by my friend Mr. Schwabe; and it is that we propose by our plan to supersede all existing schools, and render all existing school-rooms valueless. Now, it seems to me, that the plan put forward by the Church party here, seems rather to insinuate that they have caught us tripping, when they offer to avail themselves of school-rooms al-ready in existence, and assume that we contemplate doing nothing of the kind. I have mentioned a dozen times, it is my firm belief, if a system of education such as we propose were adopted, you would have no difficulty in getting an Act of Parliament for a local rate in Manchester, and in doing what your Corporation does with the water-works, taking power to use, either by purchase or renting, existing school-rooms. I do not conceal the fact from our friends, that I believe, if we have a system of rating for free schools, the effect will be to supersede all other schools, which are now partly supported upon the eleemosynary principle, that is, by charitable contributions. I do not conceal from others,—I cannot conceal from myself,—that if you establish free schools in every parish, you will ultimately close all those schools that now call upon the poor chil-dren to pay 3d. or 4d. a week, and in which the difference of ex-pense is now made up by the contributions of the congregations. If they did not have this effect, they would be unworthy of the name of national schools. But I have never considered that the school-rooms in connection with existing places of worship, or otherwise, would be rendered useless, for I have always considered they might be rented or purchased in precisely the same way as Mr. Schwabe has suggested; they might be rented for the week-time, and left on the Sunday in the hands of the congregations. This is merely a matter of detail; but we should be taking a rash leap if we had contemplated closing all existing schools, and wasting the vast capital invested in bricks and mortar for the erection of them.

Another strong objection which I have heard from our dissenting friends has been, that the secular system of education is adverse to religious teaching. I cannot tell how to account for it, but there seems to be a pertinacious resolution to maintain that the teaching the people reading, writing, arithmetic, geography, grammar, and the rest, is inimical to religion. Now, I have found the most curious refutation of this doctrine, where I have been, in the practice of the very parties who have objected to us. I remember at Birmingham, I found there a preparatory school built by a joint-stock association, by men of every religious denomination—I heard of a clergyman sending his son to that school. No religion is taught there—the building would never have been erected, unless by a compromise, which agreed that no religion should be taught in that school; and yet, the very parties that object to us for not proposing to give religion with secular education, send their sons to schools where secular education is separated, avowedly, from religious teaching. Again, in Yorkshire, I was present at a meeting where a gentleman stoutly maintained it was impossible to separate religious from secular instruction. It was in Huddersfield. And another gentleman said, "How can you possibly maintain that doctrine? You know the Huddersfield College here could not exist a day, unless we consented altogether and totally to separate religious from secular teaching; and you know you send your son to the college, and that he never received any religious instruction there!" I must say that gentleman was silent for the rest of the evening. But I also found that at Huddersfield, they have, in connection with their Mechanics' Institution, a very excellent school for young children (not for adults), where they may go and enjoy the benefits of this institution for a week, by subscribing $3\frac{1}{2}$d. They give the smallest doses of instruction, because they see the ginshops and such places offer to their customers a twopenny or threepenny taste; and so they let the children come in for a week for 3½d., in hopes that they will be tempted to repeat the dose,— I think a very wise regulation. I find there are hundreds of the children in this admirable school; but that excludes all religious teaching. I do not know whether the Bible exists in the institution library; but they never touch it in the schools, and never use it as a school-book for teaching religion. And this applies to the schools generally connected with the mechanics' institutions in Yorkshire, of the union of which my friend, Mr. Baines, is president; in those schools there is no religion taught or professed to be taught. And, therefore, in my travels, I have found that gentlemen offered in their own practice the best example of the success of our principle, and the best refutation of their own theories.

I have heard it said, the voluntary principle is succeeding very well, and that has been said by men for whose judgment in other matters I have great respect; but I am glad, among the other advantages afforded by our friends, the Church Society in this town, that we have got a corroboration of the doctrine with which we started, that the existing system of schooling is very defective. The Church party tell us, what we were aware of before, that we have a multitude of school-houses, but they are badly attended, and the instruction is not sufficiently good to attract children. The great fallacy we have hitherto had in the statistics of education is this,— we have taken school-houses for schooling, and mistaken bricks and mortar for good masters. I never doubted we have had vast efforts made in building schools; nothing is so easy as to galvanise an effort in a congregation or a district for raising a school, or to persuade men that when they have done that they have provided for education. What do bricks and mortar do for education? The gentlemen of this Church system have told us—these schools are in many cases standing idle, and the children do not come to them. I have heard mentioned, wherever I have been, that you have plenty of schools, and the people will not attend the schools until you adopt some system of compulsion, some coercive system, and compel people to send their children to school; it is of no use building schools, for the children will not attend them. I have heard this compulsory system of attendance at schools advocated in private meetings, in friends' houses, wherever I have been—where gentlemen have spoken, probably, with less reserve than they would in public; and I have found, to my astonishment, everywhere a strong opinion in favour of a compulsory attendance in schools.

Now, I beg my friends will understand that I did not bring that principle with me to Manchester. We have stopped short of that yet; and we say, before you call on us to do that, you must show us first that people will not send their children to school. You have two things to do; firstly, to establish free schools in Manchester, to receive all the children of those who may choose to send them there; and, in the next place, to have good schoolmasters. I am firmly convinced, as I have told my friends everywhere, that if you set up good schools, and have good schoolmasters, you will have no difficulty in filling your schools. I have never yet found a good schoolmaster that did not fill his school, even when the children had to pay 2d. or 3d. a week for the schooling. And if, after you had established a free school, and given every one the opportunity of attending gratis, and given them good masters, you find the people will not send their children to the schools, but bring them up in idleness and ignorance, I don't know that, under such circumstances, I should see that it would be any great infringement of the liberty of the subject, if you did adopt some plan; first, perhaps, to seduce or bribe them to send their children to school, and, if that would not do, to try a little compulsion. I don't see any objection in principle to that; but I say to our friends, before you do that, try every inducement to make them come; and I should not be squeamish about any outcry there might be of the liberty of the subject, and so on;—there is just as much liberty in Switzerland as in England, and in Switzerland they do punish parents who do not send their children to the free school, unless they can show they are giving them an education elsewhere.

These are some of the objections I have heard our friends of the dissenting bodies urge to this plan in the last few weeks. They have objected, on the ground of principle, that they cannot separate the secular from the religious education. Well, I must say we have endeavoured to be very accommodating to these gentlemen, and have found it very difficult to please them. When the attempt was for many years to have an education combined with religion, then these same gentlemen told us it was contrary to their consciences, either to receive or pay money raised by taxation, for teaching religion. When we offer to separate it, we are told by these same gentlemen, that it is contrary to their conscientious convictions to separate religious from secular teaching. I do think such a course, if persevered in, will go very far to alienate the feelings of the great mass of the working community, who, I am very much afraid (speaking of the surrounding district), are not in communion with either Dissent or Church; it will do very much, I fear, to alienate the great mass of the people from those who take an impracticable course, which stops the avenues of education to the working classes, by setting up obstacles which it is impossible for any rational man either to obviate or remove.

Now, have those gentlemen a due appreciation of the value of the education which they are opposing, apart from religious instruction? I believe they must have an adequate idea of the value of secular knowledge. I put it to them, do they not value it in their own cases and in their own families? I put it to a gentleman I met with, one of my strongest opponents,—a minister of religion,— and he told me, in a party of religious men, that "he valued secular knowledge so much, he would not give his secular knowledge, apart from all religion, in exchange for all the world." Well, and if he would not put himself on a par with the unenlightened peasant for the whole world, is he carrying out the Christian principle of doing to others as he would be done by, if he lightly interposes obstacles to the acquisition of some portion of that knowledge which he values so highly, by the great mass of his poorer fellow-countrymen? I want to ask the gentlemen, who interpose at all times the question of religion as an obstacle to secular teaching, do they or do they not consider that knowledge is in itself a good? I will say, apart from religion altogether, do they consider that Seneca or Cicero were better for their knowledge than the common gladiator or peasant of their day? But even as a matter of religious import, I would ask those gentlemen, do they not think they will have a better chance of gaining over the mass of the people of this country to some kind of religious influence, if they begin by offering to their children, and tempting their children to acquire, some kind of secular knowledge? It seems to me, that to argue otherwise would contend for this,—that ignorance and barbarism, and vice, drunkenness, and misery, are conducive to Christianity, and the opposite qualities contrary to it. I feel we are in danger of alienating the great mass of the people in these manufacturing districts from every religious communion, and even estranging their minds from every principle of Christianity, if we allow this unseemly exhibition to go on—of men squabbling for their distinctive tenets of religion, and making that a bone of contention, and a means of depriving the great mass of the people of the knowledge that is necessary for them to gain their daily bread, or to preserve themselves in respectability. Why, what a spectacle do we present to the world? Where is our boasted common sense, which we think enables us to steer our way through social and political difficulties, when we vaunt ourselves with our superiority to Frenchmen, Germans, Danes, and Italians? Where is our boasted superiority, when the American Minister can come to our Town Hall here, and taunt us with the ignorance of our people, and when nobody dares to rise up and say, we have done as much for education as they have in America? Is it not true (as Mr. Lawrence properly said), that we can show a great accumulation of wealth, that we are exporting more largely than any other nation, but there is something more wanted; and I agree with him, there is danger so long as it is wanted; and that there is no time to be lost—not a day, not an hour to be lost. I do not boast of the country we live in, so long as the mass of the people are uneducated and ignorant. Our friend, our worthy president (Mr. A. Henry, M.P.), whom I met at Leeds —and who, allow me to say, most manfully maintains your principles wherever he goes—told them at the Mechanics' Institution meeting at Leeds:—"They say we are a great nation—that is true, we are a great nation, if paying an enormous taxation, and keeping up an enormous navy, and exporting a large amount of goods, constitute greatness, we are a mighty nation; but so long as we have an ignorant people, we have not much reason to boast of our greatness."

I have nothing more to say than to exhort you, now you have encouraging symptoms of progress, to continue and agitate in the same way you have hitherto done. I have seen nothing since I joined your ranks to make me doubt you have got hold of the right principle. I don't think any other can possibly succeed in this country, that is, provided what I have heard from religious bodies for the last fifteen years be truth,—if they have been shamming, and telling us they have qualms of conscience which they have none at all,—if they have been telling us they are voluntaries, when they are looking and sighing for endowment,—then, I say, the parties who have taken up another principle may succeed, and we may fail, and I can only say I am sorry they allowed me to lose time in trying to make them take up with this. But I do not think it possible that any plan of this kind can succeed. I want you to base it on the American experience; they have gone through this ordeal, and adopted the very plan we want. I call for the American system. I do not want to have my Bible read in the schools; because, if so, the children of 60,000 people here must go uneducated. I am neither an advocate for the Bible as a school-book, nor for its exclusion as a school-book; I am for the American system precisely as it stands. And I say, now is the time for you to continue the agitation of this question, and more actively than ever. The very fact of the attention paid to what is going on in Manchester, by the press of the whole kingdom, shows to what a degree the whole kingdom looks to Manchester to solve this great and difficult question. You have had the honour of commencing this agitation; you are now met with another agitation, which is far from being an enemy or a rival, and will ultimately be an assistant. I will say,—go on—quarrel with nobody—invite their concurrence. If you will appoint me to the Conference, I shall be happy and proud to be one of a deputation to their body, to seek an interview, and ask a private and confidential conversation with the gentlemen taking the lead in this scheme. I say, don't go in opposition to anybody, but keep your own course. I believe you have got the right principle, and, if you have—I know you of old—I believe you are the right men to succeed in it.

Ten

TORY DEMOCRACY

Benjamin Disraeli

Benjamin Disraeli, Earl of Beaconsfield (1804-1881), Tory statesman, was the creator of modern conservatism in England. Early in his life he advocated in his novels an alliance between the solid worker and rural laborer and the aristocracy; he first put these principles into effect in the Reform Act of 1867. However, it was not until 1872 that he actually used these ideas as a basis for political action in a party platform. On June 24, 1872, at the Crystal Palace, in an address to the Central Society of the Conservatives, he unfolded what became known as "Tory Democracy." This political philosophy not only envisaged a natural union between the aristocracy and the working classes but also promoted imperialism and social legislation. It was largely on this platform that his party was returned to power in 1874 and he became prime minister. Disraeli understood far better than many of his contemporaries that in a democratic society it is essential to alleviate social distress and thus remove the causes of potential political revolution. Disraeli, as a reformer from above, is in the great tradition of Pitt, Burke, and Peel. "Mr. Disraeli at Sydenham," *The Times,* London, 25 June, 1872.

In the few observations that I shall presume to make on this occasion I will confine myself to some suggestions as to the present state of the Constitutional cause and the prospects which, as a great Constitutional party, are before us. Some years ago—the Tory party experienced a great overthrow. . . . Instead of those principles which were professed by Mr. Pitt and Lord Granville . . . the Tory system had degenerated into a policy which found its basis on the principles of exclusiveness and restriction. A body of public men distinguished by their capacity took advantage of these circumstances. They seized the helm of affairs . . . they endeavoured to substitute cosmopolitan for national principles; and they baptised the new scheme of politics with the plausible name of Liberalism. . . . During the 40 years that have elapsed since the commencement of this new system . . . the real state of affairs has been this: the attempt of one party to establish in this country cosmopolitan ideas, and the efforts of another . . . to recur to and resume the national principles to which we attribute the greatness and glory of this country. . . . Gentlemen, the Tory party, unless it is a national party, is nothing. . . . It is not a confederacy of nobles, it is not a democratic multitude; it is a party formed from all classes of the realm—classes alike and equal before the law, but whose different conditions and different aims give vigour and variety to our national life. . . . Now, I have always been of the opinion that the Tory party has three great objects. The first is to maintain the institutions of this country— not from any sentiment of political superstition, but because we believe that the principles upon which a community like England can alone safely rest—the principles of liberty, of order, of law, and of religion—ought not to be intrusted to individual opinion or to the caprice and passion of the multitudes, but should be embodied in a form of permanence and power. . . . We associate with the Monarchy the ideas which it represents,—the majesty of law, the administration of justice, the fountain of mercy and of honour. We know that the Estates of the Realm, by the privileges they enjoy, are the best security for public liberty and good government. We believe that a national profession of faith can only be attained by maintaining an Established Church . . . and that no society is safe unless there is a public recognition of the Providential government of the world, and of the future responsibility of man. . . . If the first great object of the Tory party is to maintain the institutions of the country, the second is, in my opinion, to maintain the Empire of England. . . . Not that I for one object to self-government . . . But self-government . . . when it was conceded, ought to have been conceded as part of a great policy of Imperial consolidation. . . . It ought to have been accompanied by an Imperial tariff . . . and . . . by the institution of some representative council in the metropolis, which would have brought the Colonies into constant and continuous relations with the Home Government. . . . Another object of the Tory party . . . is the elevation of the condition of the people. . . . The great problem is to achieve such results without violating those principles of economic truth upon which the prosperity of all States depends. . . . The attention of public men should be directed to the condition of the people . . . It concerns the state of the dwellings of the people, the moral consequences of which are not less important than the physical. It concerns their enjoyment of some of the chief elements of nature— air, light, and water. It concerns the regulation of their industry, the inspection of their toil. It concerns the purity of their provisions, and it touches upon all the means by which you may wean them from habits of excess and of brutality. . . . The people of England possess every personal right of freedom . . . [and they have] seen the time had arrived when social, not political improvement is the object at which they should aim. . . . England will have to decide between national and cosmopolitan principles. The issue is not a mean one. It is whether you will be content to be a comfortable England, modelled and moulded upon Continental principles and meeting in due course an inevitable fate, or whether you will be a great country—an Imperial country—a country where your sons, when they rise, will rise to paramount positions, and obtain not merely the respect of their countrymen, but command the respect of the world. . . . You have nothing to trust to but your own energy and the sublime instinct of an ancient people. . . . The highest . . . may lend us his greatest aid; . . . The assistance of the humblest is not less efficient. Act in this spirit and you will succeed. . . . You will deliver to your posterity a land of liberty, of prosperity, of power, and of glory.

Eleven

APPEAL FOR JUSTICE

Charles Bradlaugh

Charles Bradlaugh (1833-1891), politician and advocate of free thought, was first elected to Parliament in 1880, but as he refused to take the oaths on the Bible he was not allowed to take his seat. He was re-elected and excluded twice more; finally after a third re-election he was permitted to affirm and take his seat. His speech of June 23, 1880, was a plea for Parliament to recognize the position of those who did not accept any orthodox religious beliefs. The country had accepted Dissenters, Roman Catholics, and Jews, and after much difficulty it finally accepted atheists. Bradlaugh's acceptance into Parliament indicated that England had become, politically at least, a secular society. Parliament never claimed that Bradlaugh's election was invalid, but since the sixteenth century it had insisted on the right to determine its own membership, and Bradlaugh was excluded because he would not conform to its rules. "Four Speeches Delivered at the Bar of the House of Commons During the Parliamentary Struggle, First Speech: June 23rd, 1880," *Speeches by Charles Bradlaugh* (London, A. & H. Bradlaugh Bonner, 1902).

Mr. Speaker,—I have to ask the indulgence of every member of this House while, in a position unexampled in the history of this House, I try to give one or two reasons why the resolution which you have read to me should not be enforced.

If it were not unbecoming I should appeal to the traditions of the House against the House itself, and I should point out that in

none of its records, so far as my poor reading goes, is there any
case in which this House has judged one of its members in his
absence, and taken away from that member the constitutional right
he has. ("Hear, hear.") There have been members against whom
absolute legal disqualification has been urged. No such legal disqualification is ventured to be urged by any member of this House
against myself. But even those members have been heard in their
places; those members have been listened to before the decision was
taken against them; and I ask that this House shall not be less
just to myself than it has always been to every one of its members.
("Hear, hear.")

Do you tell me I am unfit to sit amongst you? ("Hear, hear," and
"Order, order.") The more reason, then, that this House should
show the generosity which judges show to a criminal, and allow
every word he has to say to be heard. But I stand here, Sir, as no
criminal. I stand here as the chosen of a constituency of this country, with my duty to that constituency to do. I stand here, Sir—if
it will not be considered impertinent to put it so—with the most
profound respect for this House, of which I yet hope and mean to
form a part, and on whose traditions I should not wish to cast one
shadow of reproach. I stand here returned duly; no petition against
my return; no impeachment of that return. I stand here returned
duly, ready to fulfil every form that this House requires, ready to
fulfil every form that the law permits this House to require, ready
to do every duty that the law makes incumbent upon me.

I will not in this presence argue whether this House has or has
not the right to set its decision against the law, because I should
imagine that even the rashest of those who spoke against me would
hardly be prepared to put in the mouth of one whom they consider
too advanced in politics an argument so dangerous as that might
become. I speak within the limits of the law, asking for no favor
from this House for myself or for my constituents, but asking the
merest justice which has always been accorded to a member of
the House. ("Hear, hear," and "Order.") I have to ask indulgence
lest the memory of some hard words which have been spoken in
my absence should seem to give to what I say a tone of defiance,
which it is far from my wish should be there at all; and I am the
more eased because although there were words spoken which I had

always been taught English gentlemen never said in the absence of an antagonist without notice to him, yet there were also generous and brave words said for one who is at present, I am afraid, a source of trouble and discomfort and hindrance to business. I measure the generous words against the others, and I will only make one appeal through you, Sir, which is, that if the reports be correct that the introduction of other names came with mine in the heat of passion and the warmth of debate, the gentleman who used those words, if such there were, will remember that he was wanting in chivalry, because, while I can answer for myself, and am able to answer for myself, nothing justified the introduction of any other name beside my own to make a prejudice against me. (Cheers, "Question," and "Order.")

I fear lest the strength of this House, judicially exercised as I understand it to be—with infrequency of judicial exercise—that the strength of this House makes it forget our relative positions. At present I am pleading at its bar for justice. By right it is there [pointing to the seats] I should plead. It is that right I claim in the name of those who sent me here. No legal disqualification before my election, or it might have been made the ground of petition; no legal disqualification since my election—not even pretended.

It is said: "You might have taken the oath as other members did." I could not help, when I read that, Sir, trying to put myself in the place of each member who said it. I imagined a member of some form of faith who found in the oath words which seemed to him to clash with his faith, but still words which he thought he might utter, but which he would prefer not to utter if there were any other form which the law provided him; and I asked myself whether each of those members would not then have taken the form which was most consonant with his honor and his conscience. If I have not misread, some hon. members seem to think that I have neither honor nor conscience. Is there not some proof to the contrary in the fact that I did not go through the form, believing that there was another right open to me? ("Hear, hear," and "Order.") Is that not some proof that I have honor and conscience?

Of the gentlemen who are now about to measure themselves against the rights of the constituencies of England, I ask what justification have they for that measurement? They have said that I thrust my opinions on the House. I hold here, Sir, the evidence of Sir Thomas Erskine May, and I can find no word of any opinion of mine thrust upon the House at all. I have read—it may be that the reports misrepresent—that the cry of "Atheist" has been raised from that side. [Pointing to the Opposition side.] No word of all mine before the committee put in any terms those theological or anti-theological opinions in evidence before the House. I am no more ashamed of my own opinions, which I did not choose—opinions into which I have grown—than any member of this House is ashamed of his; and much as I value the right to sit here, and much as I believe that the justice of this House will accord it to me before the struggle is finished, I would rather relinquish it for ever than it should be thought that by any shadow of hypocrisy I had tried to gain a feigned entrance here by pretending to be what I am not. (Cheers, and cries of "Order.")

On the Report of the Committee as it stands, on the evidence before the House, what is the objection to my either affirming or taking the oath? It is said I have no legal right to affirm. I will suppose that to be so. It is the first time that the House has made itself a court of law from which there may be no appeal, and deprived a citizen of his constitutional right of appeal to a court of law to make out what the statute means in dealing with him. There is no case in which this House has overridden everything, and put one of its members where he had no chance of battling for his right at all. Take the oath. It is possible that some of the lawyers, who have disagreed among themselves even upon that (the Opposition) side of the House, may be right, and that I may be wrong in the construction I have put upon the oath; but no such objection can come. There is no precedent—there is, I submit respectfully, no right—in this House to stand between me and the oath which the law provides for me to take: which the statute, under penalty even upon members of this House themselves if they put me out from my just return, gives me the right to take.

What kind of a conflict is provoked here if this resolution be enforced? Not a grave conflict in a court of law, where the judges exclude passion: where they only deal with facts and evidence. I do not mean that these gentlemen do not deal with facts; but, if I am any judge of my own life's story, there have been many things put against myself which I can hardly reckon in the category of facts. I don't mean that they are not right, for hon. members may know more of myself than I do myself; but, judging myself as I know myself, some of the members who have attacked me so glibly during the last few days must have been extraordinarily misinformed, or must have exceedingly misapprehended the matters they alleged. It has been said that I have paraded and flaunted some obnoxious opinions. I appeal to your justice, Sir, and to that of the members of this House, to say whether my manner has not been as respectful as that of man could be—whether in each case I have not withdrawn when you told me. If I now come here with even the appearance of self-assertion, it is because I would not be a recreant and coward to the constituency that sent me to represent them; and I mean to be as members have been in the best history of this assembly.

I ask the House, in dealing with my rights, to remember how they are acting. It is perfectly true that by a majority they may decide against me now. What are you to do then? Are you going to declare the seat vacant? First, I tell you that you have not the right. The moment I am there [pointing inside the House] I admit the right of the House, of its own good will and pleasure, to expel me. As yet I am not under your jurisdiction. As yet I am under the protection of the law. A return sent me to this House, and I ask you, Sir, as the guardian of the liberties of this House, to give effect to that return. The law says you should, and that this House should. And naturally so; because, if it were not so, any time a majority of members might exclude anyone they pleased.

What has been alleged against me? Politics? Are views on politics urged as a reason why a member should not sit here? Pamphlets have been read: I won't say with accuracy, because I will not libel any of the hon. members who read them; but, surely, if they are grounds for disqualification they are grounds for indictment to be proved against me in a proper fashion. There is no case in all the records of this House in which you have ransacked what a man has written and said in his past life and then challenged him with it here. My theology? It would be impertinent in me, after the utterances of men so widely disagreeing from me that have been

made on the side of religious liberty during the past two nights—
it would be impertinent in me to add one word save this. It is said
that you may deal with me because I am isolated. I could not help
hearing the ring of that word in the lobby as I sat outside last
night. But is that a reason, that because I stand alone the House
are to do against me what they would not do if I had 100,000 men
at my back? (Cries of "Oh!") That is a bad argument, which pro-
vokes a reply inconsistent with the dignity of this House, and
which I should be sorry to give.

I have not yet used—I hope no passion may tempt me to be using
—any words that would seem to savor of even a desire to enter into
conflict with this House. I have always taught, preached, and believed in the supremacy of Parliament, and it is not because for
a moment the judgment of one Chamber of Parliament should be
hostile to me that I am going to deny the ideas I have always held;
but I submit that one Chamber of Parliament—even its grandest
Chamber, as I have always held this to be—has no right to override
the law. The law gives me the right to sign that roll, to take and
subscribe the oath, and to take my seat there [pointing to the
benches]. I admit that the moment I am in the House, without any
reason but your own good will, you can send me away. That is your
right. You have full control over your members. But you cannot
send me away until I have been heard in my place, not as a sup-
pliant as I am now, but with the rightful audience that each member has always had.

There is one phase of my appeal which I am loth indeed to
make. I presume you will declare the seat vacant. What do you
send me back to Northampton to say? I said before, and I trust I
may say again, that this assembly is one in which any man might
well be proud to sit—prouder I that I have not some of your traditions and am not of your families, but am of the people, the
people that sent me here to speak for them. Do you mean that I
am to go back to Northampton as to a court, to appeal against you
—that I am to ask the constituency to array themselves against this
House? I hope not. If it is to be, it must be. If this House arrays itself against an isolated man—its huge power against one citizen—if
it must be, then the battle must be too. But it is not with the consti-
uency of Northampton alone—hon. members need not mistake—

that you will come into conflict if this appeal is to go forward, if the House of Commons is to override the statute law to get rid of even the vilest of members. Had you alleged against me even more than against one man whose name was mentioned in this House last night, I should still have held that the House cannot supersede the rights of the people. But not as much is alleged against me as was alleged against that man, in whose case the House itself said that its conduct had been subversive of the rights of the people. I beg you, for your own sakes, don't put yourselves in that position. I have no desire to wrestle with you for justice. I admit that I have used hard words in my short life, giving men the right in return to say hard things of me; but is it not better that I should have the right to say them to your faces? If they are within the law, let the law deal with me fairly and properly; but, if they are without the law, not unfairly, as I submit you are doing now.

You have the power to send me back; but in appealing to Northampton I must appeal to a tribunal higher than yours—not to courts of law, for I hope the days of conflict between the assembly which makes the law and the tribunals which administer it are passed. It must be a bad day for England and for Great Britain, if we are to be brought again to the time when the judges and those who make the law for the judges are in rash strife as to what they mean. But there is a court to which I shall appeal: the court of public opinion, which will have to express itself. You say it is against me. Possibly; but if it be so, is it against me rightly or wrongly? I am ready to admit, if you please, for the sake of argument, that every opinion I hold is wrong and deserves punishment. Let the law punish it. If you say the law cannot, then you admit that you have no right; and I appeal to public opinion against the iniquity of a decision which overrides the law and denies me justice. I beg your pardon, Sir, and that of the House too, if in this warmth there seems to lack respect for its dignity; and as I shall have, if your decision be against me, to come to that table when your decision is given, I beg you, before the step is taken in which we may both lose our dignity—mine is not much, but yours is that of the Commons of England—I beg you, before the gauntlet is fatally thrown; I beg you, not in any sort of menace, not in any sort of boast, but as one man against six hundred, to give me that justice which on the other side of this hall the judges would give me were I pleading there before them. (Loud cheers and cries of "Order," amid which Mr. Bradlaugh again bowed and retired.)

Twelve

THE ARTIST AND INTELLECTUAL AS A SOCIALIST

William Morris

William Morris (1834-1896), poet and artist, was an associate of the Pre-Raphaelite Brotherhood. In 1883 he joined the Social Democratic Federation and became an ardent socialist. Morris and his friends were intellectual and romantic socialists preaching the simple life; they were often somewhat "highbrow" for their working class associates. Morris, like Shelley before him, wrote both political treatises and socialist poetry. "The Voice of Toil," from his *Chants for Socialists,* was one of his many occasional poems written to cheer and to encourage the socialist movement. The poetry was not socialist realism but rather anti-industrial writing, expressing some hope for the future. His "May Day (1892)" was a similar poem expressing great hopes and aims; May Day, the worker's traditional day of celebration throughout the world, was thus chosen to be commemorated as a sort of international holiday. Morris' socialist poems were not written to please critics but to express what the poet called "life"; as he put it, "There is no wealth but life." While the poems may seem sentimental and somewhat forced to our more sophisticated age, it is necessary to remember that in the nineteenth century sentiment was highly approved and that Morris and his friends felt that all forms of art should be harnessed to spread the message of reform. To them the artist was definitely a part of society; he could not choose to separate himself from it. "Chants for Socialists," May Morris, editor, *The Collected Works of William Morris* (London, Longmans Green & Co., 1910-1915).

The Voice of Toil

I heard men saying, leave hope and praying,
All days shall be as all have been;
Today and tomorrow bring fear and sorrow,
The never-ending toil between.

When Earth was younger mid toil and hunger
In hope we strove, and our hands were strong;
Then great men led us, with words they fed us,
And bade us right the earthly wrong.

Go read in story their deeds and glory,
Their names amidst the nameless dead;
Turn then from lying to us slow-dying
In that good world to which they led;

Where fast and faster our iron master,
The thing we made, forever drives,
Bids us grind treasure and fashion pleasure
For other hopes and other lives.

Where home is a hovel and dull we grovel,
Forgetting that the world is fair;
Where no babe we cherish, lest its very soul perish,
Where our mirth is crime, our love a snare.

Who now shall lead us, what god shall heed us,
As we lie in the hell our hands have won?
For us are no rulers but fools and befoolers,
The great are fallen, the wise men are gone.

I heard men saying, leave tears and praying,
The sharp knife heedeth not the sheep;
Are we not stronger than the rich and the wronger,
When day breaks over dreams and sleep?

Come, shoulder to shoulder ere the world grows older!
Help lies in nought but thee and me;
Hope is before us, the long years that bore us
Bore leaders more than men may be.

Let dead hearts tarry and trade and marry,
And trembling nurse their dreams of mirth,

While we the living our lives are giving
To bring the bright new world to birth.

Come, shoulder to shoulder ere earth grows older!
The Cause spreads over land and sea;
Now the world shaketh, and fear awaketh,
And joy at last for thee and me.

May Day (1892)

THE WORKERS.

O Earth, once again cometh Spring to deliver
Thy winter-worn heart, O thou friend of the Sun;
Fair blossom the meadows from river to river
And the birds sing their triumph o'er winter undone.

O Earth, how a-toiling thou singest thy labour
And upholdest the flower-crowned cup of thy bliss,
As when in the feast-tide drinks neighbour to neighbour
And all words are gleeful and nought is amiss.

But we, we, O Mother, through long generations,
We have toiled and been fruitful, but never with thee
Might we raise up our bowed heads and cry to the nations
To look on our beauty, and hearken our glee.

Unlovely of aspect, heart-sick and a-weary
On the season's fair pageant all dim-eyed we gaze;
Of thy fairness we fashion a prison-house dreary
And in sorrow wear over each day of our days.

THE EARTH.

O children! O toilers, what foemen beleaguer
The House I have built you, the Home I have won?
Full great are my gifts, and my hands are all eager
To fill every heart with the deeds I have done.

THE WORKERS.

The foemen are born of thy body, O Mother,
In our shape are they shapen, their voice is the same;
And the thought of their hearts is as ours and no other;
It is they of our own house that bring us to shame.

THE EARTH.

> Are ye few? Are they many? What words have ye spoken
> To bid your own brethren remember the Earth?
> What deeds have ye done that the bonds should be
>   broken,
> And men dwell together in good-will and mirth?

THE WORKERS.

> They are few, we are many; and yet, O our Mother,
> Many years were we wordless and nought was our deed,
> But now the word flitteth from brother to brother;
> We have furrowed the acres and scattered the seed.

THE EARTH.

> Win on then unyielding, through fair and foul weather,
> And pass not a day that your deed shall avail.
> And in hope every spring-tide come gather together
> That unto the Earth ye may tell all your tale.
>
> Then this shall I promise, that I am abiding
> The day of your triumph, the ending of gloom,
> And no wealth that ye will then my hand shall be hiding
> And the tears of the spring into roses shall bloom.

Thirteen

THE POOR:

A PROPOSED SOLUTION

William Booth

William Booth (1829-1912), better known as "General Booth," was the founder of the Salvation Army. He was a great champion of the poor, and unlike many of his contemporaries he viewed poverty not as the consequence of sin or of improvidence but rather as a result of environment or personal misfortunate. He surveyed the situation of the poor in England and offered his own solution in his book *In Darkest England and the Way Out*. When it appeared in 1890 the book caused a great sensation, and Booth became an international figure. It is his solution to the problem of poverty that is given here. His ideas are very romantic and very much in the tradition of the imperialists who wanted to plant good Anglo-Saxon stock all over the empire. However, the very fact that he proposed an answer was in itself significant, the more so because he attacked the problem within the framework of the humanitarian tradition which had engendered reforms such as those proposed by Lord Shaftesbury earlier in the century. "Deliverance," *In Darkest England and the Way Out* (Philadelphia, Funk & Wagnalls Co., 1890).

The dark and dismal jungle of pauperism, vice, and despair is the inheritance to which we have succeeded from the generations and centuries past, during which wars, insurrections, and internal troubles left our forefathers small leisure to attend to the well-being of the sunken tenth. Now that we have happened upon more fortunate times, let us recognise that we are our brother's keepers, and set to work, regardless of party distinctions and religious differences, to make this world of ours a little bit more like home for those whom we call our brethren.

The problem, it must be admitted, is by no means a simple one; nor can anyone accuse me in the foregoing pages of having minimised the difficulties which heredity, habit, and surroundings place in the way of its solution, but unless we are prepared to fold our arms in selfish ease and say that nothing can be done, and thereby doom those lost millions to remediless perdition in this world, to say nothing of the next, the problem must be solved in some way. But in what way? That is the question. It may tend, perhaps, to the crystallisation of opinion on this subject if I lay down, with such precision as I can command, what must be the essential elements of any scheme likely to command success.

Section 1.—The Essentials to Success

The first essential that must be borne in mind as governing every Scheme that may be put forward is that it must change the man when it is his character and conduct which constitute the reasons for his failure in the battle of life. No change in circumstances, no revolution in social conditions, can possibly transform the nature of man. Some of the worst men and women in the world, whose names are chronicled by history with a shudder of horror, were those who had all the advantages that wealth, education and station could confer or ambition could attain.

The supreme test of any scheme for benefiting humanity lies in the answer to the question, What does it make of the individual? Does it quicken his conscience, does it soften his heart, does it enlighten his mind, does it, in short, make more of a true man of him, because only by such influences can he be enabled to lead a human life? Among the denizens of Darkest England there are many who have found their way thither by defects of character which would under the most favourable circumstances relegate them to the same position. Hence, unless you can change their character your labour will be lost. You may clothe the drunkard, fill his purse with gold, establish him in a well-furnished home, and in three, or six, or twelve months he will once more be on the Embankment, haunted by delirium tremens, dirty, squalid, and ragged. Hence, in all cases where a man's own character and defects constitute the reasons for his fall, that character must be changed and that conduct altered if any permanent beneficial results are to be attained. If he is a drunkard, he must be made sober; if idle, he must be made industrious; if criminal, he must be made honest; if impure, he must be made clean; and if he be so deep down in vice, and has been there so long that he has lost all heart, and hope, and power to help himself, and absolutely refuses to move, he must be inspired with hope and have created within him the ambition to rise; otherwise he will never get out of the horrible pit.

Secondly: The remedy, to be effectual, must change the circumstances of the individual when they are the cause of his wretched condition, and lie beyond his control. Among those who have arrived at their present evil plight through faults of self-indulgence or some defect in their moral character, how many are there who would have been very differently placed to-day had their surroundings been otherwise? Charles Kingsley puts this very abruptly where he makes the Poacher's widow say, when addressing the Bad Squire, who drew back

> Our daughters, with base-born babies,
> Have wandered away in their shame.
> If your misses had slept, Squire, where they did,
> Your misses might do the same.

Placed in the same or similar circumstances, how many of us would have turned out better than this poor, lapsed, sunken multitude?

Many of this crowd have never had a chance of doing better; they have been born in a poisoned atmosphere, educated in circumstances which have rendered modesty an impossibility, and have been thrown into life in conditions which make vice a second nature. Hence, to provide an effective remedy for the evils which we are deploring these circumstances must be altered, and unless my Scheme effects such a change, it will be of no use. There are multitudes, myriads, of men and women, who are floundering in the horrible quagmire beneath the burden of a load too heavy for them to bear; every plunge they take forward lands them deeper; some have ceased even to struggle, and lie prone in the filthy bog, slowly suffocating, with their manhood and womanhood all but perished. It is no use standing on the firm bank of the quaking morass and anathematising these poor wretches; if you are to do them any good, you must give them another chance to get on their feet, you must give them firm foothold upon which they can once more stand upright, and you must build stepping-stones across the bog to enable them safely to reach the other side. Favourable circumstances will not change a man's heart or transform his nature, but unpropitious circumstances may render it absolutely impossible for him to escape, no matter how he may desire to extricate himself. The first step with these helpless, sunken creatures is to create the desire to escape, and then provide the means for doing so. In other words, give the man another chance.

Thirdly: Any remedy worthy of consideration must be on a scale commensurate with the evil with which it proposes to deal. It is no use trying to bail out the ocean with a pint pot. This evil is one whose victims are counted by the million. The army of the Lost in our midst exceeds the numbers of that multitudinous host which Xerxes led from Asia to attempt the conquest of Greece. Pass in parade those who make up the submerged tenth, count the paupers indoor and outdoor, the homeless, the starving, the criminals, the lunatics, the drunkards, and the harlots—and yet do not give way to despair! Even to attempt to save a tithe of this host requires that we should put much more force and fire into our work than has hitherto been exhibited by anyone. There must be no more philanthropic tinkering, as if this vast sea of human misery were contained in the limits of a garden pond.

Fourthly: Not only must the Scheme be large enough, but it must be permanent. That is to say, it must not be merely a spasmodic effort coping with the misery of to-day; it must be established on a durable footing, so as to go on dealing with the misery of to-morrow and the day after, so long as there is misery left in the world with which to grapple.

Fifthly: But while it must be permanent, it must also be immediately practicable. Any Scheme, to be of use, must be capable of being brought into instant operation with beneficial results.

Sixthly: The indirect features of the Scheme must not be such as to produce injury to the persons whom we seek to benefit. Mere charity, for instance, while relieving the pinch of hunger, demoralises the recipient; and whatever the remedy is that we employ, it must be of such a nature as to do good without doing evil at the same time. It is no use conferring sixpennyworth of benefit on a man if, at the same time, we do him a shilling's worth of harm.

Seventhly: While assisting one class of the community, it must not seriously interfere with the interests of another. In raising one section of the fallen, we must not thereby endanger the safety of those who with difficulty are keeping on their feet.

These are the conditions by which I ask you to test the Scheme I am about to unfold. They are formidable enough, possibly, to deter many from even attempting to do anything. They are not of my making. They are obvious to anyone who looks into the matter. They are the laws which govern the work of the philanthropic reformer, just as the laws of gravitation, of wind and of weather, govern the operations of the engineer. It is no use saying we could build a bridge across the Tay if the wind did not blow, or that we could build a railway across a bog if the quagmire would afford us a solid foundation. The engineer has to take into account the difficulties, and make them his starting point. The wind will blow, therefore the bridge must be made strong enough to resist it. Chat Moss will shake; therefore we must construct a foundation in the very bowels of the bog on which to build our railway. So it is with the social difficulties which confront us. If we act in harmony with these laws we shall triumph; but if we ignore them they will overwhelm us with destruction and cover us with disgrace.

But, difficult as the task may be, it is not one which we can neglect. When Napoleon was compelled to retreat under circumstances which rendered it impossible for him to carry off his sick and wounded, he ordered his doctors to poison every man in the hospital. A general has before now massacred his prisoners rather than allow them to escape. These Lost ones are the Prisoners of Society; they are the Sick and Wounded in our Hospitals. What a shriek would arise from the civilised world if it were proposed to administer to-night to every one of these millions such a dose of morphine that they would sleep to wake no more. But so far as they are concerned, would it not be much less cruel thus to end their life than to allow them to drag on day after day, year after year, in misery, anguish, and despair, driven into vice and hunted into crime, until at last disease harries them into the grave?

I am under no delusion as to the possibility of inaugurating a millennium by my Scheme; but the triumphs of science deal so much with the utilisation of waste material, that I do not despair of something effectual being accomplished in the utilisation of this waste human product. The refuse which was a drug and a curse to our manufacturers, when treated under the hands of the chemist, has been the means of supplying us with dyes rivalling in loveliness and variety the hues of the rainbow. If the alchemy of science can extract beautiful colours from coal tar, cannot Divine alchemy enable us to evolve gladness and brightness out of the agonised hearts and dark, dreary, loveless lives of these doomed myriads? Is it too much to hope that in God's world God's children may be able to do something, if they set to work with a will, to carry out a plan of campaign against these great evils which are the nightmare of our existence?

The remedy, it may be, is simpler than some imagine. The key to the enigma may lie closer to our hands than we have any idea of. Many devices have been tried, and many have failed, no doubt; it is only stubborn, reckless perserverance that can hope to succeed; it is well that we recognise this. How many ages did men try to make gunpowder and never succeeded? They would put saltpetre to charcoal, or charcoal to sulphur, or saltpetre to sulphur, and so were ever unable to make the compound explode. But it has only been discovered within the last few hundred years that all three were needed. Before that gunpowder was a mere imagination, a phantasy of the alchemists. How easy it is to make gunpowder, now the secret of its manufacture is known!

But take a simpler illustration, one which lies even within the memory of some that read these pages. From the beginning of the world down to the beginning of this century, mankind had not found out, with all its striving after cheap and easy transport, the miraculous difference that would be brought about by laying down two parallel lines of metal. All the great men and the wise men of the past lived and died oblivious of that fact. The greatest mechanicians and engineers of antiquity, the men who bridged all the rivers of Europe, the architects who built the cathedrals which are still the wonder of the world, failed to discern what seems to us so obviously simple a proposition, that two parallel lines of rail would diminish the cost and difficulty of transport to a minimum. Without that discovery the steam engine, which has itself been an invention of quite recent years, would have failed to transform civilisation.

What we have to do in the philanthropic sphere is to find something analogous to the engineer's parallel bars. This discovery I think I have made.

Section 2.—My Scheme

What, then, is my Scheme? It is a very simple one, although in its ramifications and extensions it embraces the whole world. In this book I profess to do no more than to merely outline, as plainly and as simply as I can, the fundamental features of my proposals. I propose to devote the bulk of this volume to setting forth what can practically be done with one of the most pressing parts of the problem, namely, that relating to those who are out of work, and who, as the result, are more or less destitute. I have many ideas of what might be done with those who are at present cared for in some measure by the State, but I will leave these ideas for the present.

It is not urgent that I should explain how our Poor Law system could be reformed, or what I should like to see done for the Lunatics in Asylums, or the Criminals in Gaols. The persons who are provided for by the State we will, therefore, for the moment, leave out of count. The indoor paupers, the convicts, the inmates of the lunatic asylums are cared for, in a fashion, already. But, over and above all these, there exists some hundreds of thousands who are not quartered on the State, but who are living on the verge of despair, and who at any moment, under circumstances of misfortune, might be compelled to demand relief or support in one shape or another. I will confine myself, therefore, for the present to those who have no helper.

It is possible, I think probable, if the proposals which I am now putting forward are carried out successfully in relation to the lost, homeless, and helpless of the population, that many of those who are at the present moment in somewhat better circumstances will demand that they also shall be allowed to partake in the benefits of the Scheme. But upon this, also, I remain silent. I merely remark that we have, in the recognition of the importance of discipline and organisation, what may be called regimented co-operation, a principle that will be found valuable for solving many social problems other than that of destitution. Of these plans, which are at present being brooded over with a view to their realisation when the time is propitious and the opportunity occurs, I shall have something to say.

What is the outward and visible form of the Problem of the Unemployed? Alas! we are all too familiar with it for any lengthy description to be necessary. The social problem presents itself before us whenever a hungry, dirty and ragged man stands at our door asking if we can give him a crust or a job. That is the social question. What are you to do with that man? He has no money in his pocket, all that he can pawn he has pawned long ago, his stomach is as empty as his purse, and the whole of the clothes upon his back, even if sold on the best terms, would not fetch a shilling. There he stands, your brother, with sixpennyworth of rags to cover his nakedness from his fellow men and not sixpennyworth of victuals within his reach. He asks for work, which he will set to even on his empty stomach and in his ragged uniform, if so be that you will give him something for it, but his hands are idle, for no one employs him. What are you to do with that man? That is the great note of interrogation that confronts Society to-day. Not only in overcrowded England, but in newer countries beyond the sea, where Society has not yet provided a means by which the men can be put upon the land and the land be made to feed the men. To deal with him effectively you must deal with him immediately, you must provide him in some way or other at once with food, and shelter, and warmth. Next you must find him something to do, something that will test the reality of his desire to work. This test must be more or less temporary, and should be of such a nature as to prepare him for making a permanent livelihood. Then, having trained him, you must provide him wherewithal to start life afresh. All these things I propose to do. My Scheme divides itself into three sections, each of which is indispensable for the success of the whole.

In this three-fold organisation lies the open secret of the solution of the Social Problem.

The Scheme I have to offer consists in the formation of these people into self-helping and self-sustaining communities, each being a kind of co-operative society, or patriarchal family, governed and disciplined on the principles which have already proved so effective in the Salvation Army.

These communities we will call, for want of a better term, Colonies. There will be—

      (1) The City Colony.
      (2) The Farm Colony.
      (3) The Over-Sea Colony.

THE CITY COLONY.

By the City Colony is meant the establishment, in the very centre of the ocean of misery of which we have been speaking, of a number of Institutions to act as Harbours of Refuge for all and any who have been shipwrecked in life, character, or circumstances. These Harbours will gather up the poor destitute creatures, supply their immediate pressing necessities, furnish temporary employment, inspire them with hope for the future, and commence at once a course of regeneration by moral and religious influences.

From these Institutions, which are hereafter described, numbers would, after a short time, be floated off to permanent employment, or sent home to friends happy to receive them on hearing of their reformation. All who remain on our hands would, by varied means, be tested as to their sincerity, industry, and honesty, and as soon as satisfaction was created, be passed on to the Colony of the second class.

THE FARM COLONY.

This would consist of a settlement of the Colonists on an estate in the provinces, in the culture of which they would find employment and obtain support. As the race from the Country to the City has been the cause of much of the distress we have to battle with, we propose to find a substantial part of our remedy by transferring these same people back to the country, that is back again to "the Garden!"

Here the process of reformation of character would be carried forward by the same industrial, moral, and religious methods as have already been commenced in the City, especially including those forms of labour and that knowledge of agriculture which, should the Colonist not obtain employment in this country, will qualify him for pursuing his fortunes under more favourable circumstances in some other land.

From the Farm, as from the City, there can be no question that large numbers, resuscitated in health and character, would be restored to friends up and down the country. Some would find employment in their own callings, others would settle in cottages on a small piece of land that we should provide, or on Co-operative Farms which we intend to promote; while the great bulk, after trial and training, would be passed on to the Foreign Settlement, which would constitute our third class, namely The Over-Sea Colony.

THE OVER-SEA COLONY.

All who have given attention to the subject are agreed that in our Colonies in South Africa, Canada, Western Australia and elsewhere, there are millions of acres of useful land to be obtained almost for the asking, capable of supporting our surplus population in health and comfort, were it a thousand times greater than it is. We propose to secure a tract of land in one of these countries, prepare it for settlement, establish in it authority, govern it by equitable laws, assist it in times of necessity, settling it gradually with a prepared people, and so create a home for these destitute multitudes.

The Scheme, in its entirety, may aptly be compared to A Great Machine, foundationed in the lowest slums and purlieus of our great towns and cities, drawing up into its embrace the depraved and destitute of all classes; receiving thieves, harlots, paupers, drunkards, prodigals, all alike, on the simple conditions of their being willing to work and to conform to discipline. Drawing up these poor outcasts, reforming them, and creating in them habits of industry, honesty, and truth; teaching them methods by which alike the bread that perishes and that which endures to Everlasting Life can be won.

Forwarding them from the City to the Country, and there continu-ing the process of regeneration, and then pouring them forth on to the virgin soils that await their coming in other lands, keeping hold of them with a strong government, and yet making them free men and women; and so laying the foundations, perchance, of another Empire to swell to vast proportions in later times. Why not?

Fourteen

 # THE PROBLEM OF
THE HOUSE OF LORDS

The Earl of Rosebery

Archibald Philip Primrose, Fifth Earl of Rosebery (1847-1929) was Liberal prime minister in 1894-1895. The Liberal Party had split in 1886 over the question of home rule for Ireland; many Liberals had joined the Tories, especially the Liberal peers, who flocked to the Tories in droves. The result was a permanent Tory majority in the House of Lords. This meant that when a Tory ministry was in power everything proposed and passed in the Commons was accepted without a demur by the upper house, but when the Liberals were in power the opposite was true. This situation became very clear when the Lords rejected Gladstone's Third Home Rule Bill in 1894. Rosebery, who was certainly no radical, was much concerned for the future, as his correspondence with Queen Victoria in 1894 indicates. He foresaw that the Lords would either have to mend themselves or have their veto powers cut down in some way. Rosebery was championing the democratic electorate and the right of the people through their representatives to have laws made for their welfare. In a sense he was summing up the liberal view of the peers for the whole century. Rosebery was wiser than he knew at the time; the peers did finally reject legislation that was acceptable to the Commons in the ministry of Mr. Asquith, and the upshot was the Parliament Act of 1911 which limited their veto powers. Rosebery might well be said to have been the prophet of things to come in the next century. "Memorandum by the Earl of Rosebery, ? *March-April* 1894," and Extract from "The

165

Earl of Rosebery to Queen Victoria, 10 Downing Street, White-
hall 1st Nov. 1894," *The Letters of Queen Victoria, Third
Series, A Selection from Her Majesty's Correspondence and
Journal Between the Years 1886 and 1901* (London, John
Murray, 1931), Vol. II.

10 DOWNING STREET [? March-April 1894].

The present position of the House of Lords must be a subject
of anxiety to every one who considers the conditions and possibil-
ities of politics.

It is not too much to say that that position is, as I have said in
public more than once, a source, not of security but of danger.
I do not say that this is the fault of the House of Lords. It might
easily be argued that it is. But I wish to put that on one side, and
to confine myself to stating that in my opinion the peril of the
situation arises from circumstances beyond the control of the Peers.

In 1831 the position of the House of Lords was more attacked
than it is now. Had the Peers not yielded then with regard to the
Reform Bill they would in all probability have produced a revolution. They did yield, however, and the country turned eagerly to
the other questions then opened out, so that, partly from this circumstance, and partly from the difficulty of dealing with it, the
question of the House of Lords sank into the background. From
1832-1885 the question of the House of Lords has indeed been
mainly academical. Parties in it were pretty equally divided; the
Conservative majority was on the whole wisely led, more especially
by the Duke of Wellington; and occasions of friction were comparatively few. But in 1884 the question was anew forced upon the
country by the rejection of the Franchise Bill by the House of Lords.
There is no doubt that a very strong feeling was then produced.
The Franchise Bill * was, however, passed in the autumn of that year,
and in 1885 the House of Commons was elected on the new democratic suffrage. This was in itself a new complication in the position

---

* This bill granted universal manhood suffrage in England. It abolished the
old forty shilling franchise in the country—the towns already had virtual manhood suffrage—and democraticized England. Now the country had single member
constituencies generally and the old historic counties and boroughs were no
longer the basis for the House of Commons. The individual became the unit.
This bill ended the control of the territorial aristocracy. [Ed. note.]

of the House of Lords. For here was a Chamber elected by six millions of voters, all exulting in the exercise of their powers, which was liable to be controlled by another Chamber, not elected in any sense, not representing anybody, and one hereditary in its character.

In 1886 a further change took place, also disastrous to the House of Lords. On the subject of Home Rule for Ireland a schism took place in the Liberal Party, which threw the great mass of the Liberal Peers into the arms of the Conservative majority. So much was this the case that—in addition to the other disadvantages already referred to, the hereditary, irresponsible, and unrepresentative character of the House—there was the further embarrassment of its being practically limited to a single party. It was obvious then that, although from 1886-1892 there was no difficulty, because the same party was dominant in both Houses, when a House of Commons should be elected in which the majority should be Liberal, there would be immediately an acute conflict. This has soon come to pass. It did not take place on the rejection of the Irish Home Rule Bill because on that point there was a majority of seventy purely English Members on the side of the House of Lords. But on the occasion of the Employers' Liability Bill the opportunity was seized. Some Liberals, like Lord Farrer, for whom I have a profound respect, are of the opinion that the Peers were justified in the course they then took. If that be so, it is a conclusive proof of the strength of the feeling against the House of Lords. Because, if on a point on which people are divided, and on which the House of Lords certainly appears to be defending freedom of contract, there can be the bitterness of feeling which at present exists, it is obvious that in a dispute with the House of Commons on any great popular issue, the feeling would be overwhelming. Of the strength of the present hostility I have little doubt. Everyone who speaks in the country is astonished at it. I myself have been struck by it in the same way. The apparent slightness of the cause that elicits it is a conclusive proof of its dominant vigour.

I personally have always been in favour of a second Chamber, and was an advocate of the reform of the House of Lords. On two separate occasions I brought the question of its reform before that House, and spoke as plainly on the subject as I do now. It is possible that on those occasions, in 1884 and 1888, reform might have been effected. During the late Government it might also have been managed, but it is not now, I fear, practicable. The House of Commons are violently hostile to the idea, and so is the Liberal Party throughout the country; while the Conservatives are not friendly to it.

It is easy to understand how galling this House is to the party to which it happens to be opposed. When the Conservative Party is in power, there is practically no House of Lords: it takes whatever the Conservative Government brings it from the House of Commons without question or dispute; but the moment a Liberal Government is formed, this harmless body assumes an active life, and its activity is entirely exercised in opposition to the Government.

Therefore, while the Conservative Party is in, we have not the control of a second Chamber; but when the Liberal Party is in, it has to encounter not merely the control, but also the determined hostility of this body. It is in fact a permanent barrier raised against the Liberal Party.

I point this out to show the practical difficulty. For it is of no use to say of the House of Lords that the Peers are conscientious in their action, that they are honestly Tory and honestly Unionist, for the point of the objection is that they are so honestly of one party that they feel it is their duty on all occasions to oppose the other, a course which, however conscientious, the Government which they thus oppose naturally resents.

I have drawn up this memorandum to show exactly how the matter stands in my opinion, not to blame the Peers, or indeed to blame anybody, but to show the dangerous incompatibility of their relations with the House of Commons, and the hopelessness of the present position as regards the Liberal Party.

I cannot suggest any remedy, for any remedy which would be agreeable to the House of Commons would be revolting to the House of Lords, and any remedy which would please the House of Lords would be spurned by the House of Commons.

But it is well to look this serious situation plainly in the face: it is a permanent and not a fleeting danger to the constitution. It may be said that if the Tories came in to-morrow the question would cease to exist, for the want of harmony would then disappear. But this would only be a postponement, for the Tory Party could not hold power forever, and the feeling would simply accumulate against the coming of the next Liberal Government.

10 DOWNING STREET, WHITEHALL, 1st *Nov.* 1894.

Lord Rosebery's own view of the situation is this, that it is from the broadest point of view important to take advantage of the present opportunity. He believes that the system by which the House of Lords—now, unfortunately, owing to causes on which he will not dwell, a party organisation—controls a Liberal but not a Conservative Government is obnoxious to the conscience of the country as well as to its best interests. But he also believes that this is a moment of calm, and therefore favourable to revision. What he has always dreaded, as he has stated in public, is that the question of the House of Lords should come for decision at a crisis of passion and storm. Then the constitution would be hurriedly cast into the crucible with lamentable and incalculable results.

The policy of the Government practically comes to this, that the constitution cannot long stand the strain of a permanent control exercised by a Conservative branch of the legislature on all Liberal Governments; that it is well that this question should be decided at a peaceful juncture; and that in the issue between the House of Lords and the House of Commons the Government takes the side of the House of Commons.

Beyond this Lord Rosebery does not go.

Your Majesty will have noticed the marked way in which he asserted himself as a second Chamber man, as against many of his own party, who, unthinkingly in his opinion, declare themselves partisans of an uncontrolled House of Commons. This point is vital to Lord Rosebery; it might not be by any means vital to other Liberal Governments, . . .

Fifteen

THE BUDGET
AND THE PEOPLE

David Lloyd George

David Lloyd George (1863-1945), prime minister and reformer, was first elected to Parliament in 1890; he retained his seat until 1945. He sat as a Liberal and was reckoned by his contemporaries to be an extreme radical. When his party was victorious in 1905 he was appointed president of the Board of Trade; in 1908 he became chancellor of the Exchequer. While chancellor he introduced an old age pension scheme which was to be followed by similar reforms. As a direct consequence of the naval race with Germany the government undertook to build more "dreadnoughts"; the increased expenditure upset the national finances, and Lloyd George decided on a different sort of budget—one that shifted the burden of taxation from the producers to the possessors of wealth. After the budget was introduced on April 29, 1909, the rich landholders were furious and did all in their power to halt its acceptance. Lloyd George delivered a whole series of attacks upon his opponents, of which that delivered at Limehouse on July 30 was the most famous. His audience on this occasion were some 4,000 people crowded into the room on a scorching hot evening; the crush added to the intensity of the event. The budget was rejected by the House of Lords and this led to the constitutional crisis that was finally solved with the Parliament Act of 1911 which severely curtailed the powers of the upper house. The "Limehouse Speech" can be considered the first blast of the trumpet against the Peers; it was also the forerunner of other radical addresses expressing hostility against the rich. Lloyd George may well be thought of as the creator of the modern egalitarian Great Britain. "The Budget and the People, Limehouse, London, 30 July, 1909," *Daily Chronicle* (London, 1909), by kind permission of the late Lord Beaverbrook.

A few months ago a meeting was held not far from this hall, in the heart of the City of London, demanding that the Government should launch into enormous expenditure on the Navy. That meeting ended up with a resolution promising that those who passed that resolution would give financial support to the Government in their undertaking. There have been two or three meetings held in the City of London since, attended by the same class of people, but not ending up with a resolution promising to pay. On the contrary, we are spending the money, but they won't pay. What has happened since to alter their tone? Simply that we have sent in the bill. We started our four "Dreadnoughts." They cost eight millions of money. We promised them four more; they cost another eight millions. Somebody has to pay, and then these gentlemen say, "Perfectly true; somebody has to pay, but we would rather that somebody were somebody else." We started building; we wanted money to pay for the building; so we sent the hat round. We sent it round amongst workmen, and the miners and weavers of Derbyshire and Yorkshire,* and the Scotchmen of Dumfries, who, like all their countrymen, know the value of money; they all dropped in their coppers. We went round Belgravia, and there has been such a howl ever since that it has well-nigh deafened us.

But they say, "It is not so much the 'Dreadnoughts' we object to, it is pensions." If they objected to pensions why did they promise them? They won elections on the strength of their promises. It is true they never carried them out. Deception is always a pretty contemptible vice, but to deceive the poor is the meanest of all. They go on to say, "When we promised pensions we meant pensions at the expense of the people for whom they were provided. We simply meant to bring in a Bill to compel workmen to contribute to their own pensions." If that is what they meant, why did they not say so?

* A reference to the by-elections which took place in Derbyshire, Yorkshire and Dumfries a few days before this speech was delivered, when the main issue before the electors was the Budget which in each three divisions was supported by substantial majorities. [Ed. note.]

The Budget, as your chairman has already so well reminded you, is introduced not merely for the purpose of raising barren taxes, but taxes that are fertile, taxes that will bring forth fruit—the security of the country which is paramount in the minds of all. The provision for the aged and deserving poor—was it not time something was done? It is rather a shame that a rich country like ours —probably the richest in the world, if not the richest the world has ever seen—should allow those who have toiled all their days to end in penury and possibly starvation. It is rather hard that an old workman should have to find his way to the gates of the tomb, bleeding and footsore, through the brambles and thorns of poverty. We cut a new path for him—an easier one, a pleasanter one, through fields of waving corn. We are raising money to pay for the new road —aye, and to widen it so that 200,000 paupers shall be able to join in the march. There are many in the country blessed by Providence with great wealth, and if there are amongst them men who grudge out of their riches a fair contribution towards the less fortunate of their fellow-countrymen they are very shabby rich men.

We propose to do more by means of the Budget. We are raising money to provide against the evils and the sufferings that follow from unemployment. We are raising money for the purpose of assisting our great friendly societies to provide for the sick and the widows and orphans. We are providing money to enable us to develop the resources of our own land. I do not believe any fair-minded man would challenge the justice and the fairness of the objects which we have in view in raising this money.

Some of our critics say, "The taxes themselves are unjust, unfair, unequal, oppressive—notably so the land taxes." They are engaged, not merely in the House of Commons, but outside the House of Commons, in assailing these taxes with a concentrated and a sustained ferocity which will not allow even a comma to escape with its life. Now, are these taxes really so wicked? Let us examine them; because it is perfectly clear that the one part of the Budget that attracts all this hostility and animosity is that part which deals with the taxation of land. Well, now let us examine it. I do not want you to consider merely abstract principles. I want to invite your attention to a number of concrete cases; fair samples to show you how in these concrete illustrations our Budget proposals work. Let us take them. Let us take first of all the tax on undeveloped land and on increment.

Not far from here, not so many years ago, between the Lea and the Thames, you had hundreds of acres of land which was not very useful even for agricultural purposes. In the main it was a sodden marsh. The commerce and the trade of London increased under Free Trade, the tonnage of your shipping went up by hundreds of thousands of tons and by millions; labour was attracted from all parts of the country to cope with all this trade and business which was done here. What happened? There was no housing accommodation. This Port of London became overcrowded, and the population overflowed. That was the opportunity of the owners of the marsh. All that land became valuable building land, and land which used to be rented at £2 or £3 an acre has been selling within the last few years at £2,000 an acre, £3,000 an acre, £6,000 an acre, £8,000 an acre. Who created that increment? Who made that golden swamp? Was it the landlord? Was it his energy? Was it his brains— a very bad lookout for the place if it were—his forethought? It was purely the combined efforts of all the people engaged in the trade and commerce of the Port of London—trader, merchant, shipowner, dock labourer, workman—everybody except the landlord. Now, you follow that transaction. Land worth £2 or £3 an acre running up to thousands. During the time it was ripening the landlord was paying his rates and his taxes not on £2 or £3 an acre. It was agricultural land, and because it was agricultural land a munificent Tory Government voted a sum of two millions to pay half the rates of those poor distressed landlords, and you and I had to pay taxes in order to enable those landlords to pay half their rates on agricultural land, while it was going up every year by hundreds of pounds through your efforts and the efforts of your neighbours.

That is now coming to an end. On the walls of Mr. Balfour's meeting last Friday were the words, "We protest against fraud and folly." So do I. These things I tell you of have only been possible up to the present through the "fraud" of the few and the "folly" of the many. What is going to happen in the future? In future those landlords will have to contribute to the taxation of the country on the basis of the real value—only one halfpenny in the pound! Only a halfpenny! And that is what all the howling is about.

There is another little tax called the increment tax. For the future what will happen? We mean to value all the land in the kingdom. And here you can draw no distinction between agricultural land and other land, for the simple reason that East and West Ham was agricultural land a few years ago. And if land goes up in the future by hundreds and thousands an acre through the efforts of the community, the community will get 20 per cent. of the increment. Ah! what a misfortune it is that there was not a Chancellor of the Exchequer to do this thirty years ago! We should now have been enjoying an abundant revenue from this source.

I have instanced West Ham. Let me give you a few more cases. Take cases like Golder's Green and others of a similar kind where the value of land has gone up in the course, perhaps, of a couple of years through a new tramway or a new railway being opened. Golder's Green to begin with. A few years ago there was a plot of land there which was sold at £160. Last year I went and opened a tube railway there. What was the result? This year that very piece of land has been sold for £2,100—£160 before the railway was opened—before I went there—£2,100 now. My Budget demands 20 per cent. of that.

There are many cases where landlords take advantage of the needs of municipalities and even of national needs and of the monopoly which they have got in land in a particular neighbourhood in order to demand extortionate prices. Take the very well-known case of the Duke of Northumberland, when a county council wanted to buy a small plot of land as a site for a school to train the children who in due course would become the men labouring on his property. The rent was quite an insignificant thing; his contribution to the rates I think was on the basis of 30s. an acre. What did he demand for it for a school? £900 an acre. All we say is this—if it is worth £900, let him pay taxes on £900.

There are several of these cases that I want to give to you. Take the town of Bootle, a town created very much in the same way as these towns in the East of London, by the growth of a great port, in this case Liverpool. In 1879 the rates of Bootle were £9,000 a year—the ground rents were £10,000—so that the landlord was receiving more from the industry of the community than all the rates derived by the municipality for the benefit of the town. In 1898 the rates had gone up to £94,000 a year—for improving the place, constructing roads, laying out parks, and extending lighting and opening up the place. But the ground landlord was receiving in ground rents £100,000. It is time that he should pay for all this value, and the Budget makes him pay.

Another case was given me from Richmond which is very interesting. The Town Council of Richmond recently built some workmen's cottages under a housing scheme. The land appeared on the rate-book as of the value of £4, and, being agricultural, the landlord only paid half the rates, and you and I paid the rest for him. It is situated on the extreme edge of the borough, therefore not very accessible, and the town council naturally thought they would get it cheap. But they did not know their landlord. They had to pay £2,000 an acre for it. The result is that instead of having a good housing scheme with plenty of gardens and open space, plenty of breathing space, plenty of room for the workmen at the end of their days, forty cottages had to be crowded on two acres. If the land had been valued at its true value, that landlord would have been at any rate contributing his fair share of the public revenue, and it is just conceivable that he might have been driven to sell at a more reasonable price.

I do not want to weary you with these cases. But I could give you many. I am a member of a Welsh county council, and landlords even in Wales are not more reasonable. The police committee the other day wanted a site for a police station. Well, you might have imagined that if a landlord sold land cheaply for anything it would have been for a police station. The housing of the working classes —that is a different matter. But a police station means security for property. Not at all. The total population of Carnarvonshire is not as much—I am not sure it is as great—as the population of Limehouse alone. It is a scattered area; no great crowded populations there. And yet they demanded for a piece of land which was contributing 2s. a year to the rates, £2,500 an acre! All we say is, "If their land is as valuable as all that, let it have the same value in the assessment book as it seems to possess in the auction-room."

There was a case from Greenock the other day. The Admiralty wanted a torpedo range. Here was an opportunity for patriotism! These are the men who want an efficient Navy to protect our shores, and the Admiralty state that one element in efficiency is straight shooting, and say: "We want a range for practice for torpedoes on the coast of Scotland." There was a piece of land there which had a rating value of £11 2s., and it was sold to the nation for £27,225.

And these are the gentlemen who accuse us of robbery and spoliation!

Now, all we say is this: "In future you must pay one halfpenny in the pound on the real value of your land. In addition to that, if the value goes up, not owing to your efforts—if you spend money on improving it we will give you credit for it—but if it goes up owing to the industry and the energy of the people living in that locality, one-fifth of that increment shall in future be taken as a toll by the State." They say: "Why should you tax this increment on landlords and not on other classes of the community?" They say: "You are taxing the landlord because the value of his property is going up through the growth of population, through the increased prosperity of the community. Does not the value of a doctor's business go up in the same way?"

Ah, fancy their comparing themselves for a moment! What is the landlord's increment? Who is the landlord? The landlord is a gentleman—I have not a word to say about him in his personal capacity —the landlord is a gentleman who does not earn his wealth. He does not even take the trouble to receive his wealth. He has a host of agents and clerks to receive it for him. He does not even take the trouble to spend his wealth. He has a host of people around him to do the actual spending for him. He never sees it until he comes to enjoy it. His sole function, his chief pride is stately consumption of wealth produced by others. What about the doctor's income? How does the doctor earn his income? The doctor is a man who visits our homes when they are darkened with the shadow of death; who, by his skill, his trained courage, his genius, wrings hope out of the grip of despair, wins life out of the fangs of the Great Destroyer. All blessings upon him and his divine art of healing that mends bruised bodies and anxious hearts. To compare the reward which he gets for that labour with the wealth which pours into the pockets of the landlord purely owing to the possession of his monopoly is a piece—if they will forgive me for saying so—of insolence which no intelligent man would tolerate.

So much then for the halfpenny tax on unearned increment. Now I come to the reversion tax. What is the reversion tax? You have got a system in this country which is not tolerated in any other country in the world, except, I believe, Turkey—a system whereby landlords take advantage of the fact that they have got complete control over the land to let it for a term of years, spend money upon it in building, and year by year the value passes into the pockets of the landlord, and at the end of 60, 70, 80, or 90 years the whole of it passes away to the pockets of a man who never spent a penny upon it. In Scotland they have a system of 999 years lease. The Scotsmen have a very shrewd idea that at the end of 999 years there will probably be a better land system in existence, and they are prepared to take their chance of the millennium coming round by that time. But in this country we have 60 years leases. I know districts—quarry districts—in Wales where a little bit of barren rock on which you could not feed a goat, where the landlord could not get a shilling an acre for agricultural rent, is let to quarrymen for the purpose of building houses at a ground rent of 30s. or £2 a house. The quarryman builds his house. He goes to a building society to borrow money. He pays out of his hard-earned weekly wage contributions to the building society for 10, 20, or 30 years. By the time he becomes an old man he has cleared off the mortgage, and more than half the value of the house has passed into the pockets of the landlord.

You have got cases in London here. There is the famous Gorringe case. In that case advantage was taken of the fact that a man had built up a great business. The landlords said in effect, "You have built up a great business here; you cannot take it away; you cannot move to other premises because your trade and good will are here; your lease is coming to an end, and we decline to renew it except on the most oppressive terms." The Gorringe case is a very famous case. It was the case of the Duke of Westminster. Oh, these dukes, how they harass us!

Mr. Gorringe had got a lease of the premises at a few hundred pounds a year ground-rent. He built up a great business there as a very able business man. When the end of the lease came he went to the Duke of Westminster, and he said, "Will you renew my lease? I want to carry on my business here." The reply was, "Oh, yes, I will; but only on condition that the few hundreds a year you pay for ground rent shall in the future be £4,000 a year." In addition to that Mr. Gorringe had to pay a fine of £50,000, and to build up huge premises at enormous expense, according to plans approved by the Duke of Westminster.

All I can say is this—if it is confiscation and robbery for us to say to that duke that, being in need of money for public purposes, we will take 10 per cent. of all you have got, for those purposes, what would you call *his* taking nine-tenths from Mr. Gorringe?

These are the cases we have to deal with. Look at all this lease-hold system. This system—it is the system I am attacking, not in-dividuals—is not business, it is blackmail. I have no doubt some of you have taken the trouble to peruse some of those leases, and they are really worth reading, and I will guarantee that if you circulate copies of some of these building and mining leases at Tariff Reform meetings, and if you can get the workmen at those meetings and the business men to read them, they will come away sadder but much wiser men. What are they? Ground rent is a part of it—fines, fees; you are to make no alteration without somebody's consent. Who is that somebody? It is the agent of the landlord. A fee to him. You must submit the plans to the landlord's architect, and get his consent. There is a fee to him. There is a fee to the surveyor; and then, of course, you cannot keep the lawyer out. He always comes in. And a fee to him. Well, that is the system, and the landlords come to us in the House of Commons, and they say: "If you go on taxing reversions we will grant no more leases." Is not that hor-rible? No more leases, no more kindly landlords, with all their retinue of good fairies—agents, surveyors, lawyers, ready always to receive ground rents, fees, premiums, fines, reversions. The landlord has threatened us that if we proceed with the Budget he will take his sack clean away from the hopper, and the grain which we are all grinding in order to fill his sack will go into our own. Oh, I cannot believe it. There is a limit even to the wrath of outraged landlords. We must really appease them; we must offer up some sacrifice to them. Suppose we offer the House of Lords to them?

Now, unless I am wearying you I have just one other land tax to speak to you about. The landlords are receiving eight millions a year by way of royalties. What for? They never deposited the coal in the earth. It was not they who planted those great granite rocks in Wales. Who laid the foundations of the mountains? Was it the landlord? And yet he, by some divine right, demands as his toll—for merely the right for men to risk their lives in hewing those rocks—eight millions a year!

I went down to a coalfield the other day, and they pointed out to me many collieries there. They said: "You see that colliery. The first man who went there spent a quarter of a million in sinking shafts, in driving mains and levels. He never got coal, and he lost his quarter of a million. The second man who came spent £100,000 —and he failed. The third man came along and he got the coal." What was the landlord doing in the meantime? The first man failed; but the landlord got his royalty, the landlord got his dead-rent—and a very good name for it. The second man failed, but the landlord got his royalty.

These capitalists put their money in, and I asked, "When the cash failed, what did the landlord put in?" He simply put in the bailiffs. The capitalist risks, at any rate, the whole of his money; the engineer puts his brains in; the miner risks his life. Have you been down a coal mine? I went down one the other day. We sank down into a pit half a mile deep. We then walked underneath the mountain, and we had about three-quarters of a mile of rock and shale above us. The earth seemed to be straining—around us and above us—to crush us in. You could see the pit-props bent and twisted and sundered, their fibres split in resisting the pressure. Sometimes they give way, and then there is mutilation and death. Often a spark ignites, the whole pit is deluged in fire, and the breath of life is scorched out of hundreds of breasts by the consuming flame. In the very next colliery to the one I descended, just a few years ago, 300 people lost their lives in that way; and yet when the Prime Minister and I knock at the doors of these great landlords, and say to them: "Here, you know these poor fellows who have been digging up royalties at the risk of their lives, some of them are old, they have survived the perils of their trade, they are broken, they can earn no more. Won't you give something towards keeping them out of the workhouse?" they scowl at us. We say, "Only a ha'penny, just a copper." They retort, "You thieves!" And they turn their dogs on to us, and you can hear their bark every morning.

If this is an indication of the view taken by these great landlords of their responsibility to the people who, at the risk of life, create their wealth, then I say their day of reckoning is at hand.

The other day, at the great Tory meeting held at the Cannon Street Hotel, they had blazoned on the walls, "We protest against the Budget in the name of democracy, liberty, and justice." Where does the democracy come in in this landed system? Where is the liberty in our leasehold system? Where is the seat of justice in all these transactions? I claim that the tax we impose on land is fair, is just, and is moderate. They go on threatening that if we proceed they will cut down their benefactions and discharge labour. What kind of labour? What is the labour they are going to choose for dismissal? Are they going to threaten to devastate rural England by feeding and dressing themselves? Are they going to reduce their gamekeepers? Ah, that would be sad! The agricultural labourer and the farmer might then have some part of the game that is fattened by their labour. Also what would happen to you in the season? No week-end shooting with the Duke of Norfolk or anyone. But that is not the kind of labour they are going to cut down. They are going to cut down productive labour—their builders and their gardeners—and they are going to ruin their property so that it shall not be taxed.

The ownership of land is not merely an enjoyment, it is a stewardship. It has been reckoned as such in the past, and if the owners cease to discharge their functions in seeing to the security and defence of the country, in looking after the broken in their villages and in their neighbourhoods, the time will come to reconsider the conditions under which land is held in this country. No country, however rich, can permanently afford to have quartered upon its revenue a class which declines to do the duty which it was called upon to perform since the beginning.

I do not believe in their threats. They have threatened and menaced like this before, but in good time they have seen it is not to their interest to carry out their futile menaces. They are now protesting against paying their fair share of the taxation of the land, and they are doing so by saying: "You are burdening industry; you are putting burdens upon the people which they cannot bear." Ah! they are not thinking of themselves. Noble souls! It is not the great dukes they are feeling for, it is the market gardener, it is the builder, and it was, until recently, the small holder. In every debate in the House of Commons they said: "We are not worrying for ourselves. We can afford it, with our broad acres; but just think of the little man who has only got a few acres"; and we were so much impressed by this tearful appeal that at last we said: "We will leave him out." And I almost expected to see Mr. Pretyman jump over the table when I said it—fall on my neck and embrace me. Instead of that, he stiffened up, his face wreathed with anger, and he said, "The Budget is more unjust than ever."

We are placing burdens on the broadest shoulders. Why should I put burdens on the people? I am one of the children of the people. I was brought up amongst them. I know their trials; and God forbid that I should add one grain of trouble to the anxieties which they bear with such patience and fortitude. When the Prime Minister did me the honour of inviting me to take charge of the National Exchequer at a time of great difficulty, I made up my mind, in framing the Budget which was in front of me, that at any rate no cupboard should be barer, no lot should be harder. By that test, I challenge you to judge the Budget.

READING LIST

Adamson, John William, *English Education, 1789-1902* (London, 1930).

Beer, Max, *A History of British Socialism* (New York, 1950).

Brinton, Crane, *English Political Thought in the Nineteenth Century,* 2nd ed. (Cambridge, Mass., 1949; Harper paperback ed.).

——, *The Political Ideas of the English Romanticists* (London, 1926).

Butler, James Ramsey Montagu, *The Passing of the Great Reform Bill* (New York, 1914).

Cameron, Kenneth Neil, *The Young Shelley: Genesis of a Radical* (London, 1951; Collier paperback ed.).

Cruikshank, Robert James, *Charles Dickens and Early Victorian England* (London, 1949).

Fay, Charles Ryle, *Life and Labour in the Nineteenth Century* (Cambridge, 1947).

Finer, Samuel Edward, *The Life and Times of Sir Edwin Chadwick* (London, 1952).

Halevy, Elie, *A History of the English People in the Nineteenth Century,* 6 vols. (London, 1949; Barnes and Noble paperback ed.).

Hammond, John Laurence LeBreton and Barbara, *The Age of the Chartists, 1832-1854* (London, 1930).

Hutchins, B. L. and Amy Harrison, *A History of Factory Legislation* (London, 1911).

Jones, Thomas, *Lloyd George* (Cambridge, Mass., 1951).

Maccoby, Simon, *English Radicalism, 1762-1785* (New York, 1955).

Meynell, Esther Hallam, *Portrait of William Morris* (London, 1947).

Quennell, Peter, ed., *Mayhew's London* (London, 1958).

Ramsay, Anna Augusta Whittal, *Sir Robert Peel* (London, 1928).

Webb, Sidney and Beatrice, *English Poor Law Policy* (London, 1910).

Woodham-Smith, Cecil Blanche, *Florence Nightingale, 1820-1910* (London, 1950; Avon paperback ed.).

Young, George Malcolm, *Victorian England: Portrait of an Age* (London, 1936; Oxford paperback ed.).

50403

50403